THEY CALL US THE SCREAMERS

The History of
Atlantis Primal Therapy Commune,
Burtonport, Co. Donegal

Jenny James

Caliban Books

Published by Caliban Books
13 The Dock, Firle, Sussex BN8 6NY

ISBN 0 904573 27 3

Typesetting by
Eager Typesetting Company, 22a Westbourne Place, Hove, East Sussex

Reproduced from copy supplied
printed and bound in Great Britain
by Billing and Sons Limited
Guildford, London, Oxford, Worcester

THIS BOOK IS DEDICATED TO

REBECCA, my daughter, Princess of Atlantis

CONTENTS

ATLANTIS was a city and a country
An old philosopher saw,
Rising from the depths of the ages,
Obedient to love's ancient law.
They say Atlantis perished and drowned,
I can tell you that is a lie.
Atlantis still lives in Ireland
For those who can still laugh and cry.

Atlantis is a wide open country
And you're on the frontier now.
Here if you really want to grow tall,
You can grow tall as you will allow.

But growth is a dangerous business,
As sore as an hour on the rack;
For you can't put sanity and love in a package
And carry them home in a sack.
An apple's skin is tough,
And if you want to bite through to the core,
You have to have the strength and wisdom
To obey love's ancient law.
For Atlantis is soft as a peach
And tough as a frontier town,
It offers the pleasures of life
To those who are ready to drown.

There's a price to be paid
For the peace that we give:
You have to give all of yourself
If you want to live.
And when you've left
The dying West
And quit the Valium Shore,
When you've taken the chain
From your quivering brain,
You can't go back any more.

No Atlantean can recross the frontier
No visa can take you through;
For when you've lived in Atlantis,
You can't find a country new.
Our extradition writs have currency
Every place in the wide wide world;
They'll find the tiniest crack
Where you lie curled.

For once you've truly eaten,
You can only consume the best,
And when you've truly slept,
There's no other way to rest.
And everywhere you go
In the dead cold world of No,
There's no way that you can hide
If to yourself you've lied.

For Atlantis is soft as a peach
And tough as a frontier town,
It offers the pleasures of life,
But are you ready to drown?

Cos Brother, I've got to remind you,
And Sister, you've got to believe,
You can check out of Atlantis any old time,
But you can never actually leave.

For when you belong to Atlantis,
It's out of the question to part,
For it has a permanent hold
On your inner self, your guts and your heart.

For Atlantis is only a mirror
Held up to show you your face
And to try to flee your own footsteps
Is a doomed and futile race.

Spacetime is always circular
And however far you flew,
Eventually the mighty continuum
Shows you a coloured picture postcard
Of You.

Jeremy Ward

★ ★ ★

"Atlantis may be all around us and may be entered through certain window areas of dimensional interpenetration. Don't be in a hurry to find such an ultradimensional door, however: a single day in Atlantis may be equal to a month, a year, a decade, on our own space-time continuum."

Brad Steiger, p. 137
"Atlantis Rising"

PREFACE

They Call Us The Screamers will answer a lot of the questions aroused in people's minds by the numerous press and TV reports of the mysterious 'Screamers' communes. I know that in publishing my story, I will be confirming many people's prejudices, but I hope also to get across the richness, excitement and pain of living to the full, as well as the courage needed to follow one's feelings completely, wherever they may lead. Our way of life is revolutionary and arouses strong antagonism, fear or enthusiasm in those who hear about us, meet us or live with us. One thing we never meet with is indifference.

This book has not been 'written', but has been collected and selected from the wealth of letters that travel to and from Atlantis and our 'embassy' in London. These writings arise naturally out of our tribal life together, and the moods in them range from the everyday to the cosmic, from hilarity to despair, from the heat of love and optimism to the cold of bitterness and hatred. We are actually quite ordinary people – everyone has these feelings. Our difference is that we deliberately uncover, expose and explore them. My hope is that many readers who are dissatisfied with their lives, will find the encouragement in this book to begin to dare to bare themselves to their friends and associates, thereby helping to reverse the overwhelming tradition today of secrecy, politeness, half-truths and dishonesty in our dealings with one another, especially within the family circle. My belief is that 'civilized' human beings have taken a pathological path : one which leads ever further away from our real feelings and instincts, and ever closer to the destruction of our planet. The bottling up of pain and poison inside ourselves and the stifling of our love impulses simply does not work: twisted and thwarted, our feelings overspill in one way or another – on to our children and animals, into pollution and warfare, cancer and car crashes, or they stagnate in barren, boring lives.

At ATLANTIS, we have brought back colour and natural drama into everyday living. Our activities and way of being may appal or appeal, but one thing is for sure: you'll be moved to your core and highly entertained.

★ ★ ★

In the letters which unravel this tale, you will meet with terms and concepts that may seem strange to you – like 'therapy' and 'groups' and 'going into feelings' and 'facing oneself' and 'cutting off'. All these expressions simply refer to our tribal habit, which is the essence and basis of our community, of exploring in depth every wave of emotion that sweeps through our lives. To this end, we gather our people together regularly – sometimes daily – to sort out hassles, get help to investigate what we are feeling or to 'push' someone who is closing up emotionally on himself and others. Sometimes we are very heavy with one another, for we take what we do and what we stand for very seriously and no-one who persistently 'blocks' on communication is allowed to stay with us. We argue that dishonesty is what most of the world is about and they can go and live in it elsewhere! The result of our way of life is an enormously accelerated rate of personal growth and enlightenment, an energy-level which even our enemies would have to admit they have never seen equalled anywhere else, a magnificence and breadth of experience usually only experienced vicariously in the cinema – and an awful lot of people who once called themselves friends running away! This is a price we willingly pay, for the reward is more precious than 'careful' friendship: as an Atlantean, you know who you are, what you want, where you are going; you can never be a 'pushover', you feel your outline, have your feet planted fairly and squarely on the ground and own your own skin completely; you never sell out or compromise for short-lived emotional 'goodies' and you discover you are a magnificent being full of magic and colour – as long as you're willing to face the blackness and despair that must be gone through to clear yourself of all blocks.

Only a tiny minority of people have the courage to take this ideal to the limit. Because the limit means standing utterly alone against the multitude for the sake of one's own personal truth. So ATLANTIS deals with a seeming paradox: we advocate searching your soul and standing up for your truth even though this may alienate everyone you now call 'friend' – and yet one of the results of doing this is that you can experience a closeness that you previously only dreamed was possible. It's not really a contradiction: what most people call closeness is often a pretence, a compromise based on a hundred secret thoughts and impulses. Such uneasy peace does not satisfy me, or the hundreds of people who come to Atlantis each year to learn as much as they are ready to take of their own truth.

INTRODUCTION

'WRITE the history of Atlantis,' my publisher said to me. I gulped, wriggled internally, took a deep breath, and gave in. OK, I said, cursing and blessing him simultaneously. It's September 1979. I found this place in September 1974. I was looking for a country retreat, a place to hide away with my small tribe and rest from years of running an open-house anti-psychiatry centre in London; a house of our own where we couldn't be harrassed by jealous landlords. A large house we wanted, tucked away in the wilds of the Irish countryside, away from the mainstream of life, without neighbours; an anonymous sort of a place where we could do our thing without being disturbed: grow our food, bring our kids up without schools, walk naked in our gardens, carry on with our own development through therapy; perhaps offer therapeutic help quietly and privately to a select few who would not live with us.

Five years, three television programmes, three books and umpteen dozen newspaper reports later, Atlantis is famous throughout Ireland. 'The Screamers' they call us. And I'm supposed to sit here and tell you how it happened. What happened to my quiet private little nudist colony? How did we end up the most feared and famed growth centre, enlightenment centre, energy centre this side of the Atlantic? How did a bunch of atheists end up contacting extraordinary psychic abilities? How come, having ostensibly retired from politics, we are thrown once more into the forefront of the political arena when enormous Uranium finds are made in this remote little corner of Donegal, bringing with them the threat of the whole area suddenly being devastated with radioactivity and 'development'. And how come, having determined to settle forever on our wee offshore island, Inishfree, we now believe we have to remove ourselves lock, stock and barrel, from these unsafe shores, unless we are to see this Atlantis like the previous one sink beneath the waves?

Concrete thought patterns restrict my brain. Is it OK to tell them, I just 'knew' to come to Ireland? How will I explain to a sane audience that I found this house in just three days and collected £12,000 from nothing in just six weeks, and ended up affecting the lives of thousands in just five years? Sensation stories are silly, they are for the Sunday papers. Atlantis is a legend; the things that happen here just don't happen. Everyone knows that magic is dead; it's for kids; pity we can't believe in it, but we've got more sense this century.

A female Charlie Manson I've been called; or Satan's daughter; a coven leader; or a brothel keeper. A hippie cult they've called us; drop-outs, they think we take drugs; mad, loonies. A violent place that, I wouldn't go there. But thousands do. They come and find JJ is a skinny worried dark woman, sometimes full of fun, sometimes fierce; mostly quite quiet. They feel cheated: 'I thought this was supposed to be the Screamers'. Stay a day. Or two. Then they soon see why they call us that. Crazy place. Some people collapse and cry with relief to find us; others run so fast you'd think our bees were after them; some saunter off having managed not to get involved. Many people return. Most don't. We carry on.

Who are we? What do we do? Why Atlantis?

Yes, why did the name Atlantis come to me in my kitchen in the English Lake District? 'Because the house is on the Atlantic', I thought. Huh! A likely story.

★   ★   ★

The most scary thing about being first is that everyone hates you. The most scary thing about telling the truth is that no-one believes you. The most scary thing about pushing all your friends to the limit is that eventually they turn against you. The most scary thing about going all the way to get what you want regardless of obstacles is that you grow bigger and wiser and stronger; and the most scary thing about growing big and wise and strong is that people hold you in awe and only a few dare to get close.

Here I sit in Atlantis, terrified. Terrified of my own mortality, of my age (37 and I can't stop it, each year I'm a year older, and more aware of how I've unlived my life in the past). Terrified of my terror of death; not just my own death, but the death of my animals, the death of this planet. I have been obsessed with this fear since I reached consciousness around the age of eight or nine. Terrified of pain and death; I can't imagine that everyone isn't the same, but they tell me they're not. I am supposed to be a giver of life; I tell people how to live, I show them how to live. I do it well, and people are always grateful to me, even though they hate my guts at the time. Even my worst enemies have a begrudging respect for me. And yet here I sit small and terrified and huge; huge in what I have taken on, huge in what I demand of myself and of the people of Atlantis. We have taken on the end of the world. Boring, you might say, all the crank religious groups have been talking like that for centuries. Well, we hope we're wrong; but for now we're putting all our energy into preparing for the end of the world. Good lord, that's a negative sort of way to live, isn't it? Not if what you're doing is training yourself, straining yourself to the limit to become self-reliant in every important aspect of life, and encouraging everyone else to do the same. When the nuclear war comes; or when the planet tilts; or when the pollution finally overcomes us all, there will be a few groups on Earth who are ready. We are one of them. And our work, apart from getting ourselves ready, is to get as many other people ready as possible. If everyone gets ready, it won't happen. That would be nice.

But as everyone who tries to do anything decent or revolutionary in this world knows, there are rather a lot of people intent upon digging their own graves, settling down snugly to an early death, and using up everything around them without regard to the overall health of our planet. Deep down, nearly everyone knows we've had it; that this species is done for. We keep on praying it isn't true. Perhaps the 'experts' will step in at the last minute; surely they won't really blow us up; surely 'they' will sort out all this pollution business. Surely *we* don't have to do anything.

But they won't; and we do.

Jen, you're supposed to be telling them about the beginning of Atlantis, not about the end of the world.

Oh yes. I used to hate grass. I wouldn't walk through Holland Park in London when my boyfriend, Jerry, wanted me to. It made me feel bad. I preferred the car fumes. They fitted in better with what I felt inside. Years later, healthier, and living in the Lake District, another boyfriend of mine, Steve, preferred to sit in his dark, smoke-filled bedroom on a bright sunny day rather than outside our back door by the stream. 'I like London,' he said, 'it fits better what I feel inside.' Here on the West Coast of Ireland, I sit by my peatfire in September writing to you all, rather than be sailing our seas to our island, or working out there on the land to get ready for winter. I prefer the snug anxiety of working with my head; the wind and the rain bring out too much the terror that is inside me.

I am a waste product of the 20th century, just like you. I am a derelict. Instead of smoking, or drinking, or watching telly, or rushing off to the office, I am delving into the end of the world, the end of the world that is inside each one of us. Oh, they hate me for it, all of them who come near me for long. I don't blame them. But we all know it's true; the End of the World is in our hands; well, actually, I think it's already slipped through our hands. It'll be every man for himself; but we're making an all-out effort to get people together before we all go together.

Living out here in Donegal, you feel things clearer. On Inishfree Island, you feel them clearer still. Can you imagine doing without all your present entertainment, work, pastimes? Can you imagine putting yourself somewhere isolated with a group of strangers, living, laughing, loving, crying, fighting with them, just to see what happens?

That's Atlantis; that's what we do. But it's not a game, or an experiment. It's not an anthropological survey from which we can return to 'civilization'. We know that everything that happens in the world is represented in each one of us: the Vietnamese who chuck the Boat People into the sea; the Americans who tried to burn the Vietnamese off the face of the earth; the Red Indians who handed over their land to the white people; the Jews who let themselves be led into the gas chambers; the Germans who ran the camps – murderer and victim, equally responsible, it's in all of us. Facing it sometimes seems impossible. But it's better facing it around the fire or in the kitchen or up on the peatbogs together, than going through the lessons on the battlefield, in the hospitals, in the factories. Better admit what's inside us and go through the horrors about it, rather than repeat it again and again and again, century by century. It's too late anyway, it's too late to learn the slow way; we have to learn the quick way now.

So Atlantis is a growth centre. Fast growth, enforced growth. People can run away from themselves, but the world is round, and guess where they come back to? Atlanteans stand up and say, 'Yes, we have found a way that works. We have found a route back to ourselves, back to health; we have found a way to live on this planet without destroying it.'

But that's boring! All the religions say that, all the political systems say that . . .

Break while I dance around the room, assuring my audience (one person) that I can't go on with the book, that I am mad, that I have nothing to say, that I'm a charlatan, who am I to be writing this book or any other, except perhaps one entitled, 'They Call Us The Screamers – One Woman's Trip Through Paranoid Delusions.'

★ ★ ★

OK, let's go inside and have a look and see what this damned Atlantis place is made of . . .

1975

ATLANTIS YEAR ONE: SPRING

I was angry with my friend:
I told my wrath, my wrath did end.
I was angry with my foe:
I told it not, my wrath did grow.

And I watered it in fears,
Night and morning with my tears;
And I sunned it with smiles,
And with soft, deceitful wiles.

And it grew both day and night,
Till it bore an apple bright;
And my foe behold it shine,
And he knew that it was mine.

And into my garden stole
When the night had veiled the pole:
In the morning, glad I see
My foe outstretched beneath the tree.

William Blake (1757-1827)

★   ★   ★

One rainy day in Autumn 1974, I arrived in Dungloe.
Co. Donegal, in waterproof trousers and an anorac, feeling
scruffy and awkward and fighting off depression. It was four
o'clock on the third day of my search to find a new home base
for our community, which was housed meanwhile in rented
accommodation in the English Lake District. I had never been
to Southern Ireland before, but sensed that this would be the
place to find a house and land at a price we could cope with.

In Dungloe, I stopped several passers-by to ask if there was
an estate-agents in the town. They didn't know what I meant.
In a pessimistic frame of mind, I went to the Post Office to post
an optimistic letter I'd written earlier to my friend Babs back
home, and prepared to move on to the next town. I asked one
more time: 'Do you know of an estate agent in Dungloe?'
'Do you mean an auctioneer?' 'Yes, that'll do!' I was directed
down to Campbell's. The fact that it turned out to be a grocery

store didn't put me off at all. After all, the estate agent in Strabane had trebled up as a butcher's and hairdresser's.

Mr. Campbell settled comfortably to turn through the pages of his property book. I dripped water all over his floor. His wife brought me tea and cake in delicate chinaware. I relaxed a little and peeled off a few layers of steaming mountain gear. Evidently it wasn't too weird in this country for house-seekers to turn up looking like homeless tramps.

First, I was offered a roofless cottage for £1,000. Thinking of our rather large communal family, I said, 'We-ell, I had been thinking of something a little bigger.' 'And about what price were you thinking of?' Nervously recalling my £300 in the bank, I gulped and replied, 'In the region of £10,000.' 'Oh, well now . . .'

Half an hour and a few 'phone calls later, I was sitting wined and dried and a little more confident in the plush seat of Mr. Campbell's car, while he and his son drove me along the coast of Ireland. I knew, looking at the inlets and rocks and the water so blue everywhere, that in spite of this not being even remotely the kind of green and sheltered place I'd envisaged for our new tribal base, and in spite of there being so many ugly modern buildings splattered haphazardly everywhere, I'd 'come home' and that the house I was about to see just had to be the right one for us.

We drove to an old rambling palace of a place, the sort of house I'd maybe lived in in some former life-time. Reality was starting to slip away, but I had enough hold on it to know that this was going to be my home.

Back at the estate agent's office, I 'phoned Babs in England. 'Babs, I'm buying a house for £12,000. It's got eighteen rooms. I'm signing now, OK?'

That night, I trembled alone in a 'Bed and Breakfast'. I couldn't sleep. I sat up nearly all night writing letters to friends, relatives and acquaintances telling them about the house and our plans to set up a therapeutic community and asking them for loans of money. I knew that if my friends back home didn't support me, I was in a mess. But I also knew that I wasn't going to fail, because everything felt so right.

I hitched back to the Lake District pleased with myself and gaining energy from my own daring and cheek, expecting to be acclaimed and carried high on the shoulders of my cheering friends for my great deed. Huh! Four miles from our village, I 'phoned home to ask for a lift. My twelve-year-old daughter Becky answered and said no-one could come. Strange. I got home and found the house unusually silent, though I knew everyone was in. They were all hidden in their rooms.

I rooted them out and it turned out that everyone had discovered a lot of bad feelings about me while I'd been away – Babs hated me for reasons she never did face me with; Pete was jealous of me because he had failed on a similar house-seeking mission to Scotland; he 'didn't want to be taken over' he said, and anyway what kind of a place was Ireland to live in? My boyfriend Steve hated me anyway! Only my Becky responded with true delight and the hugs I needed so badly.

I still knew I had performed a miracle and that it had taken me only three days. It took me till four in the morning to get out of the others what was wrong. After that, it took me fifteen minutes to instil in them the enthusiasm I felt for our beautiful house in Burtonport.

We had one month to get the money. Pete had £3,500, accumulated in the days when he had been a doctor; another Pete had £2,000. We obtained an extension of a couple of weeks to pay the money off, and we made it. Our smallest contribution was a gift of £30, which meant as much as one carefully-drawn-up loan of £1,000. We did it, by the hundreds here and the thousands there. Thank you Steve and Jerry and Alan and Annie and Pete Hulme's aunts and Pete Judge's parents and my own stepfather and my sister and Nic Carr-Saunders and myself and Pepe, my ex-husband with your international money orders, £36 at a time, sign of love and enthusiasm and trust. And thank you Babs and Alex for the letters you wrote that didn't bring any funds but which were as much a part of the founding of Atlantis as were Pete's visits to his bank manager.

Atlantis was born midst trials and hassles and interpersonal tussles, but for me, it was firm and secure from the day I crossed the frontier at Strabane and wrote this to Babs, before I'd even heard of Burtonport:

"Dear Babs,

Did you ever see the film, 'The Wizard of Oz'? You know, the girl walks through a door and suddenly the black and white film changes to colour? Well, that's what it's like crossing the border from Northern Ireland to Eire.

As soon as I'm past the soldiers (who recognized my accent – they were from my home town, Dartford in Kent), the magic settled on me: silence. Warm mist, rough roads, no traffic; cottages crumbling back into the earth they came from; blackberry hedges all around, their fruit big and soft and ripe. Fuschia bushes growing wild.

This is the end of my journey. Only collecting Becky and my furniture could induce me ever to leave County Donegal. Picture the Lake District stripped of every car and tourist and Notice and Rule and fence. You still won't have any idea of the gentle throbbing energy of this north-west coastline speckled with islands and deserted sandy bays; a sea you can look to the bottom of, turquoise at the edges, and now and then a cottage with grass growing in its hair. This evening, I walked on an immense beach of deserted sand. I felt that all my life, all the bad times, were worth living through for this one day.

love, Jen."

Between finding Atlantis in September 1974 and moving in on 10th April, 1975 – the day before my 33rd birthday – I lived in London helping to find, set up, clear out and renovate a big squatting-house, which was to be our city 'embassy' for several years. Babs and Pete meanwhile settled into Atlantis and started giving therapy there.

When I moved to Ireland for good, the delight of actually owning my own walls for the first time in my life took hold of me, and I started painting them – astrological signs and murals all over the outside and inside of the house. I suppose that's when we really moved into Burtonport. Some local people praised them highly; many were probably horrified. The County Council tried to get me to paint the house a 'monochrome' once more. I said 'No' and never heard another word.

Meanwhile, enquiries were coming in from all over the place about our therapy. It seems we weren't the only people in the world that recognized the radical need to get to grips with the emotional distress that is like a plague on our planet.

24th April, 1975
To my ex-therapist
"Dear David,

You ask how come I left England. Well, here was this beautiful house standing empty, pregnant with potential on this rocky, misty island. I had to make a decision. It took me roughly three seconds.

So here I am for life, Queen of the Risen City of Atlantis, with my Prime Minister Clive organizing the realm; Gino, my personal guru and court jester – he's a nineteen-year-old Italian Cockney – and Phil, the palace gardener. Phil will take long months of slow melting to come out. I asked him not to leave when his money runs out this week, but to stay and carry on his good work. A little chunk of ice fell from his face as he said, 'thank you.' Gino is five feet five of blunt wisdom. His simple probes have sent me more than once into the deep pools of my beginnings. He gives me so much and yet he has come to *me* for help. He stands depressed, warming himself by the peat-range, and I know no advice for him.

Frank lives here too. He is thirty years old and until recently was still living with his Italian mother. He does excellent physical jerks with his strong body, walks eight miles to and fro Dungloe most days, but never a feeling stirs in him, so he says. So we abandon therapy sessions, he just lives here, sharpening our knives, mending hammer-handles, building me a perfect hanging wardrobe and studying greenhouse building, while my own plans stretch into the future in the shape of a goatery, a chickenery, and a pony stable. As I wrote in a letter yesterday, practical phantasy is my talent.

In our rocky garden, you can stand and gaze at the crows settling on the ruins of an old British coast-guard station next door; or you can stare out to sea, watching the strange strips of cloud over the Atlantic, and the frills of islands and inlets so interwoven that you don't know where the sea begins and Ireland ends.

Ladders up against the front of my house declare: I have conquered my fear of heights and have painted an artistic but badly-spaced ATLANTIS sign above the door. Now, dear local people, I am afraid you are due for rather a surprise as I am going to paint the whole of the vast frontage of our house in a six-month mural of zodiac signs and planet symbols and under-water plants and waving hair and hands and eyes and whatever else surges up from my unconscious.

At six o'clock every day, I risk my life. I am giving sessions to a borderline psychotic who threatens every day to become less borderline. We can't let him live in the house. It is a hateful job; I feel I am giving birth to a devil, and I have to screw up all my life-energy to do it; but it is a big challenge to me and I like that. I won't let him kill me, but I have to use all my control in order to keep him at bay. How come the psychotics I meet are always six feet tall and musclebound?

At Stranraer as I was coming over here, I whiled away the boat-waiting time by throwing the Tarot. I got a quite astound-ingly favourable spread predicting prosperity, harmonious relationships, fertility, abundance and creativity – the last card actually showed a pen, a paintbrush and a recorder (which I'm training myself to play). I have the feeling that the Tarot is a realm of magic I'll explore more one day. At present, I just gather twigs from its borderlands when I need to rekindle my fire.

Jen."

25th April, 1975
To my daughter
"Dear Becky,

I'm writing to you lying bare in our sunlit garden. I don't have any particular boyfriend at the moment, I'm just happy making my room and the house beautiful and seeing everyone working and finding their place in the world. The front of our house is changing daily. I'm making a slow start – I'm a bit scared of local reaction, especially as it looks like witchcraft, all the signs of the Zodiac and symbols of the planets.

Don't worry at all about going to school out here. If the schools are anything like Babs' kids say, I wouldn't want you to go. And when I read your letters and see how good and natural they are and realize how school would have ruined that in you, I am glad you never went. If it interests you to have a look at the inside of an Irish school, that's fine, just for the experience, but you know if you hate it, you can leave immediately.

Here comes Clive with a picnic. It was lovely hearing from you. I hope you write some more soon.

love, Jen."

2nd May, 1975
To an old friend at our London Commune in Villa Rd., Brixton
"Dearest Alex,

I am very excited by your letter received just now. I'm zinging all over and can't wait for the post to take these words back to you. I just want to say I love you and all of our London Commune. I love what I spawned with you and the others and the goodness and love that is coming of it because it was born in defiance and love of ourselves and I'm very happy and I hope you all have an ecstatic time on this planet before we move on to the next one, and if dope and drink and orgies help you to ecstasy, DO IT.

I want lots more letters from you, down ones and up ones and round-the-mulberry bush ones, and I'm really glad to hear that everyone is broken up with everyone else, because then there's lots of room for movement; comings and goings and movings and growings and hassles and tussles and livings and lovings: definitely it's the only way, I know that now; everything else is boring: my love and my juiciness are never so great as when I've just broken up with someone, then I can look at them and fancy them with the greatest cheek and no strings or duties or expectations, just relating out of a vibrant sexuality and the totally unsquashable sauce that turns me on and makes me love myself.

I'm working myself to a frazzle here and it's giving me more and more time to live, the more I work, the more I get done, and the more hours there are in every day, still time for loads of sex and long conversations with Gino on the state of the Cosmos, and loads of fights and jokes with Clive and even time to try and help Dave cry, plus hours and hours spent writing thousands of letters. I love it. I do my thinking – because I'm a planner and philosopher you know – during the sessions when I'm supposed to be working on these stuck people. They think the sessions have got something to do with therapy, but of course they don't realize it's in the kitchen that their growth really takes place.

Jen."

8th May, 1975
To an ex-mate
"Dear Jerry,

Believe it or not, I feel quite friendly towards you, and would like you to make the time to come out here. We could share some beautiful sea and sky and rocks, a lovely garden where we sunbathe naked and a great house full of good people, sometimes a very quiet place, other times humming with life.

I'm giving about four therapy intensives at the moment, learning a lot and giving of my very soul. I feel I'm working in a casualty unit where people with mangled bodies are expecting a three-week cure. Part of their cure is discovering life takes more than three weeks to live.

A few days ago, I was crying in gratitude to you for a time when you saved my life when I had gone dead, by pouring cold water on my neck. You saved me that time with a natural thoughtless intuition, about water and bodies and forgetting all about therapy techniques, just seeing that a miserable baby needs energy to feel better.

It has become obvious to me that growth is not just a matter of 'going into' things, but of coming out of them too – of Healing. Nourishment is basic to healing, and you can't be nourished without good friends.

love, Jen."

In June 1975, there occurred the first of the Atlantis 'leavings' – that is, someone – in this case a young man called Anthony, who had been deeply and fruitfully involved in his own exploration of himself – suddenly disappeared. I loved Anthony, but his leaving was not just a personal loss to me, but rather a 'philosophical' jolt. How could someone who understood so well what it is we are up against, how we have to fight the whole of thousands of years of twisting inside us, who was getting on so well with opening up and finding out about himself, suddenly drop out? Little did I know then that over the Atlantean years to come, the 'leaving syndrome' would become a phenomenon that we would not only learn to expect, but end up laughing about, making up songs and poems about, and even encourage people to do! In 1975, I was not naive about the enormity of world-damage we were trying to undo in people, but I was certainly very naive in my hopes of commitment from each person. Personal revolution was something I passionately believed in myself, but it was to take me a long time before I

understood the forces at work in people to draw them back into
a world of security, obscurity and comfort.

To a girlfriend
"Dear Babs,

Anthony left here yesterday, just walked out of a session and
left. And I am left trembling all over, torn between anger and
hurt. It'll take me a few days to sort my head out. I don't know
what I'd do without Joan at this time, because she is so clear.
I am in danger of the earth slipping from under me, torturing
my brain with pointless questions like, 'Did I treat him right?'
She keeps reaffirming that everything we all did was right and
good.

I just want to get over to the London Commune as soon as
possible and pour some of the enormous energies that have been
released in me, into helping you with whatever you have under-
taken there. Please receive me and use me well.

Jen."

"Dear People of Atlantis,

I'm going to Villa Road (the London Commune) and closing
the door to escape. I don't know what I can do or say to clear
this mess that I'm lost in. I could see you were giving a lot and
I couldn't feel it. I ran away from it. It dawns on me day by day
how secret and hidden I am, and I'm scared. I don't understand
all the shit I threw out at everyone to keep myself from feeling.
How can I receive anything that's given when I feel like just
living is stealing?

Thank you for your letters. I realize you're still giving – giving
me the truth.

love, Anthony."

3rd June, 1975
"Dear Babs,

Clive is a grotty heap at the moment and this morning pulled
the following number: before we were all up, he goes down to

the bottom of the garden where there is a neighbouring house, and he howls and screams and bawls, all on his own, and unbeknown to us. First we know of it, is a policeman and one irate neighbour at the door. I was out; Gino dealt with it. Neighbour was so angry he wouldn't listen to a word of explanation or apology. He said his mother had been so disturbed she had to take tranquilizers. He was generally threatening, suggesting vague ways in which we would 'cop it'. The policeman was more open, and willing to listen.

Joan went to the house an hour ago in best middle-class style – she's excellent on such occasions – but was met with blanket hostility. They don't like 'the types' coming to our house; 'all the locals' mistrust us, and 'we'd see' what would happen.

I'm not sorry this has come to a head. Trouble was inevitable sooner or later. I'm feeling really political and ready for a fight and not in the least bit intimidated. All my visions of the locals charging up here with pitchforks and hounding us from town or burning me at the stake were obviously not far removed from reality, but now I don't feel scared in the least, just licking my lips at the thought of battle.

Jen."

30th June, 1975
"To Gino in London:

Here is my report on the latest piled-up garbage clearance campaign at Atlantis!

Arriving at Holyhead on my way back from our London Commune, and wanting a foretaste of the delighted welcome I'd be getting at home, I 'phoned to announce my imminent arrival. Frank answered, in extra-clicking, ticking mood. 'Good. Right. Yes. See you. Goodbye.' 'Hang on a minute, Frank,' says I, 'Let me use up my three minutes.' 'Now, Jenny,' says he ominously, 'Let's end this on a friendly note.' 'What are you talking about, Frank? What's up? Why haven't you written?' 'I can't tell you anything now, I'll speak to you when you get here.'

It took me hours to get over the bad vibes of this 'phone call.

Becky and I arrived at Atlantis; the commune's battered old car passed us near the house, full of smiling faces. I was suspicious. Indoors, the smiling faces were all around, and I couldn't look at any one of them. Dave's new girlfriend Shani made dinner and put candles on and the lights out. I couldn't bear it. Dave came up to me to greet me, but I didn't meet his greeting. Frank wanted to hug me, but I said, 'No, I want to know what was wrong with you on the 'phone.' Clive wanted to talk in a minimal decibel monotone about Compendium Bookshop. I couldn't look at him. Shani was shining and rosy and grinning all over the place, but I wasn't going to respond to someone I didn't know.

I was starting to think there must be something wrong with me: I am just a nasty woman, feeling rejected and not taking the friendship offered by all these nice people with their candle-light and Beatle music. I went into the kitchen and said, 'I can't stand the tension, I want a house group.' We went to the therapy room. I said I felt that Dave and Clive and Frank were scared of me. I got into a yelling match with Clive who felt 'hounded' by me; he said he felt I was Asking for something from him, that I wanted a Closeness with him he was not prepared to give. I said, What a surprise, yes, I am demanding something of you, that you MOVE out of your present blanked-out state, and surprise surprise, yes, I do want closeness from someone who was my friend and that I used to sleep with.

The whole group was spent on Clive and his yellings and body-wagglings and nothing real shifting, and it was very late, and I was tired and I said we'd carry on in the morning.

In the morning, there was Dave sitting crocheting on the sunny lawn, and everything right with the world, so it seemed. Except that I was going mad inside, furious that it was up to me again to get everyone to face what was going on. Eventually, another group was got together, and the whole of it was spent on Dave. It turned out he was terrified of me coming home, and that when he pounced up to me grinning and welcoming me, he really hated me.

And then it came out that Shani had hated me even before meeting me because of the 'effect' I was having on the menfolk. And Frank was full of gripes about having had to 'look after' Clive after I'd been severe with him on the 'phone from London. So all the smiles and candlelight had been as false as I'd sensed.

On the evening of this second day, another group was called after I'd thrown a fit in the kitchen, telling Clive to leave. He had delivered one of his popeyed purple anger reactions, clumping his fists down on the cups, then recovering himself and retreating into a white largactilite state once more, a shroud of silence hastily pulled over him. However, they 'forgot' to invite me to this group 'by mistake'. I heard it going on by chance, looked in to see what the noise was, thought I was going mad when I saw the whole house assembled there; 'phoned Babs in London to check out that I was still sane, and went into the group. Clive was not in there. I surged upstairs. He was wrapped in a heap on his bed. I told him to get to the group or leave the house. He said he'd leave the next day. I said, NO, NOW. I wasn't going to suffer another moment of death in the house. He wouldn't shift. I said I would smash him and his room up if he didn't go. I chucked a couple of armchairs at him and went for him. He held my wrists to stop me and I threatened to kick him in the balls, and I meant it. He went whiter than the sheets and started packing.

The house felt cleaner and so did I. I woke up next morning feeling better, then thought of Dave and my heart sank. He was 'working on things' in the groups, but it was getting him nowhere. He hated me, but used terror to keep his hate away. He couldn't breathe or move or be himself in my presence he said. I told him he'd better go then. He left after two days. His girlfriend stayed. There are a lot of problems with her, but at least she's alive and taking risks.

Frank had in no way resumed our former contact. I tried to get him to speak, to find out what was wrong. I spent hours of patience and love and play on him. I didn't feel angry with him, just terribly frustrated. I took off his clothes, poured water on

him and chucked pages of a Mr. World magazine all over him.
I asked him to ask me to sleep with him. He said he likes sleeping alone. I gave up, depressed. I was in the middle of being
depressed when in walked Phil, all the way from London. We
slept together and our bodies were beautiful together, but he
said he didn't want sex. The next day, when I prodded and
probed, it finally came out that he thinks sex is 'violent' and he
doesn't want anything to do with it. It was pointed out to him
that it just might be that sex makes him feel violent, but he wasn't
ready to see this. The next night, when I am sad and crying
about all the guys who are frightened of me, in comes Frank
chivalrously in the middle of the night and offers his arms to
'comfort me'. That's one way of doing what he wanted to do
anyway!

Well, the only reason I'm writing all this to you now, dear
Gino, is that I am at present ecstatically happy, and that's a
pretty good reason for recounting the saga of misery and
blockage which awaited me at Atlantis when I got home.

Goodbye for now, and I hope you move a lot while you're
away in London, because I couldn't stand you moping around
like you used to. This whole house is full of energy again now
and everyone is working magnificently hard and we are going
to have to make our living from this earth and no messing about,
so don't come back until you've sorted out your anger which
prevents you from giving your whole energy lovingly to work, not
as a chore, but as totally as you would want to make love to a
woman. I love you, but I will fight every bit of Slug in you.
I want Atlantis to be cleanly and clearly for those who know how
to live. I love your humour and your talents and our talks about
the cosmos; but this will not make up for the deadness in your
eyes and the sullenness around the corners of your mouth and
the motherbound maggotiness oozing out of your aura. So get
cleaned up, there is a New Age here, a rigid boundary to cross,
on the other side of which is real freedom, not the freedom of
groovily glossing over grot, but the freedom that comes after

discipline. No more woolly edges at Atlantis! No more slugs and snails and slowmovers!

I have faced so much hate and loss and heartbreak and sorrow and standing alone and taking fatal risks, losing all and gaining nothing but clarity, that my attitude towards others who do not do these things is becoming more and more intolerant. I have fought for my body and for my home and I have lost all my friends over and over again. No fear of loss can ever hold me back now, and no love or friendship, however dear – and yours has been very dear – can stop me now from demanding total flow and movement and NO MORE STAGNATION IN THE RISEN CITY OF ATLANTIS, so get your finger out, Gino, and don't dare come home before you've done your homework. This is not a therapy centre for mental patients, it is a recovery unit for the city survivors who want to live and already know how to. With love and fierceness, Jen."

"Dear Jen, (from Clive)

I'm a coward. I ran away. I'm an aggressive bastard at that. I'm so afraid and ashamed to show my face at Atlantis or the London Commune. I'm no longer going to be such a passive resentful aggressor, expecting everyone else to pour their energy into me to sort me out. It doesn't work, and no more will I let it happen. I've left therapy until I take full responsibility for my own growth. I'm not happy. I've left and lost you and the others, real friends like I've never known before. When I want to grow, I shall return, show my shit openly, reach out for a real relationship with you, reach out openly for the help I need, instead of just taking, sucking, leeching, and not giving.

Frank, I feel bad about the way I stubbornly refused to let in to me the love and friendship you gave to me as you tried to dissuade me from running away. If and when I return to take charge of my own destiny, I'll ask back for the friendship with you I threw away.

Clive."

★ ★ ★

27th October, 1975
Dream

"I am in a crowded house, a squatting-type place. Clive's parents have come to visit us there. His mother is pale and largactilized, and his father is dark and tense and repressed and bossy. It is a therapy commune and they have come to visit us in a resentful, guarded, withheld kind of way. There is an assumption that the woman is the mental patient, the freaked-out one, and that the man is capable and in charge. There are several visiting cynics around, social workers maybe, or observer-type psychologists, or I.S. politicoes, all very sophisticated.

I am being soft, hospitable and naive, pretending to accept all these visitors as bona fide, openly talking to them about what we do and how we do it, deliberately ignoring their blatant sarcastic hostility, their cynical, patronizing curiosity.

Suddenly, there is a freakout: 'Clive's father' explodes, goes stark-raving crazy in a psychopathic breakdown. He bursts out, his rage coming forth blindingly; he rushes like a crazed animal uncontrollable through the house. He is quite capable of murder. There is panic. I half-identify with those who want to 'phone for an ambulance immediately to get him taken away, in fact I threaten him with it myself as he is going crazy and using his madness to be irresponsibly violent. But another side of me is stronger, and I feel determined to work with this man, dangerous though he is. I yell at him enough to get through his insanity and say to him: 'Do you want me to help you? I can stop you going into a mental hospital; it's up to you. It's not easy, but it can be done.'

A glimmer of what I'm saying goes through to his brain. He is grinning and crazy and threatening, but somewhere inside him, he is pleading, he doesn't want to be put away and he does want help.

Meanwhile, dozens more of these pale, bigheaded social-worker type observers have filed in. They seem to be acquaintances of the mad middle-aged man from the time when he was calm and repressed and normal. They are there in a jeering, challenging way, as if to say, 'Let's see what this witch-doctor is up to then, let's see what kind of self-delusion she's into.' And yet there is an air of curiosity about them as if they'd rather like to see a spectacle in spite of their cynicism.

I am concentrating on the patient, trying to ignore the crowds of watchers jostling and moving about and passing to and fro and chatting and joking and passing comments. I am fighting to keep a space on a mattress to work with this man. I stare intently into his dark manic eyes and I keep his gaze and I pour all my energy and power into holding him, convincing him, urging him forward. I insist that he come nearer to the mattress, that he kneel on a cushion and not freak around the room wasting his energy. I tell him to let out his violence on the bed, to hit down with his fists. I keep urging him, saying, 'I know it seems freaky, crazy, but do it, do it and you'll see how it works, you'll see how much clearer and better you feel.' I am aware of the smug, jeering, sneering attitude of the onlookers, and how they'll be thinking, 'What simplistic nonsense is this, how can she be so naive and taken-in.' I ignore them, knowing I am right.

Finally, the man does let out loads of his violence and energy through his fists on to the bed. He is sweating and hot and surprised. He doesn't really know what he's doing or why, he is in such a swirling haze of passion, but there is still an instinct in him to get help, he is desperate and confused and my insistence gets through to him. He is not cynical like the others, because he is maddened and crazy and therefore innocent like a child.

After some time of letting off his energy, when the comments of the onlookers are getting louder and more cynical, the man says quietly to me, with amazement around his eyes and sweat on his lips, 'I do feel better.' I am heartened and close to him in communication and I ignore the white people around me. I remain strict and urgent with this man saying, 'You'll need three-hour sessions every single day. I will work with you every day for a week. I can help you. Do this week, and then make up your own mind at the end of it whether you want to go on.'

Next thing I remember is being downstairs. I am feeling slightly guilty because I have the messianic thought: 'I have to prove that I can work with a psychotic, that it is possible to get through, that I can do it where no-one else can.' I am aware that I will have to expend my whole energy, my whole soul, that I may burn myself out in the process, that there is no real reward for me, but something drives me on. I am anxious and determined, and I am worried that if I leave this man alone even for a few minutes while I am downstairs, he will have been reindoctrinated and taken over once more by the reasonable people who will convince him that I am crazy, a charlatan, living in cloud cuckoo land and that I can never succeed."

★ ★ ★

10th November, 1975
"To ATLANTIS HOUSE, Burtonport
from DONEGAL COUNTY COUNCIL

It has come to the notice of the County Council that premises which were at one time Sweeney's Hotel, Burtonport, have in recent months come to be used as an Institution for the care of persons suffering from various degrees of mental disability. It has also been noted that the front and sides of the premises are brightly painted with fishes, etc.

I am to inform you that the carrying out of works for the improvement and other alterations of any structure which materially affect the external appearance of the structure so as to render such appearance inconsistent with the character of the structure or of the neighbouring structures and the change of use of the premises requires planning permission under the Local Government Act 1963.

I am enclosing herewith an application form for planning permission together with a leaflet which sets out the information/ documents to be submitted with the application, to be completed by you for the retention of the above described unauthorized development . . .   Yours sincerely,
County Secretary."

RHYMES, TALES AND REPORTS
OF SOME OF THE
'persons suffering from various degrees of . . .'

Ian's Tale, 25th November, 1975

"Hitching through Ireland, looking at the map, it was right somehow that Atlantis was away on the west coast. It felt like coming to the end of the world. There was nothing beyond it but the sea.

I spent my first night in Burtonport in a bed and breakfast in a room six by eight feet, with a double bed in it. In the dark, it felt like a coffin, but I choked back my tears like I had for the previous twelve years and gave myself a headache instead.

Years and years of silent loneliness inside me. Years spent hating what they were doing to me but never letting on. Keep it in, stick it all down. Keep the lid on at all costs or it'll get worse. They'll really come for me – tell me I'm insane. So far my father's only labelled me half-way there: 'There's a name for people like you – neurotic.'

Guilt-ridden sexual fantasies – thrill, shame, and fear all together. Too much anxiety. Repress it. Don't feel the pain. I held on to everything, even my sperm. Went off into my head – fantasize, construct a world where people don't hate me. Where people want to know about my sensitivity, gentleness and love, and my anger, hurt and sadness, not just my academic record.

'If you ever bring home another report card like that, you'll get a damn good thrashing.' 'You know your trouble, you're just bone lazy.' While fantasies of jumping in front of a 'bus drilled through my brain. Fantasizing talking to a sympathetic psychiatrist because you were allowed to tell them you wanted to kill yourself. I never told a soul. I talked about football and politics and died inside.

Terrified of going near a woman. Feeling depraved for wanting one. Finding solace in my sister's clothes. Dying every day. Wanting love and finding deadness, I became an adequate per-

former. I passed exams and more exams. I sat in my room and
stared at the walls. Totally conned. Aged 17, I wrote: 'My
Christ, I'm going mad. I once almost convinced myself I was
mad and even now I think I'm queer. More thoughts come and
add to my unhappiness, and yet I shouldn't be unhappy. I have
a good education, good parents. I'm far better off than many.
What is it does it? At times I hate and despise myself. I know
what I want to do but I'm not good or tough enough. In the
midst of this, I have to work for Highers. How can I? I don't
want to do that kind of work. To me it's unimportant. This is
what's important for me: my state of mind; and it's terrible and
has been for four-and-a-half years.'

But somehow, something kept living deep down.

They went too far. I slowly began to give up hoping for anything from them. Their shit just got too vast and I began to trust
myself. I started to envisage other ways of being. Growing
instead of stunting. Happiness instead of fear. Freedom instead
of performing. And I began to tell people how I felt. Very
cautiously. And one or two of them responded. I kept disappearing back into my depressive mire for their tentacles were
very deep, but slowly I began to live. The damage was enormous
though. My body was almost wholly dead. I'd cut off and gone
into my brain to survive and even that wasn't too clear.

Disasters with females – feelings erupting, violence and terror
at the emptiness inside me. Fantasies of sticking my head
through windows. Conning the doc out of loads of sleepers.
The lid wouldn't go back on like before. Panic – drink, smoke,
get stoned, trip, rush about, talk, fantasize, travel, work. Not
enough. And then, bored, leafing through Peace News. Ying!
Electric vibes: 'Primal therapy. Contact Jenny James, 12 Villa
Road, London.' Blink, stare, disbelief. Fumble in pocket. 'How
much?' '10p.' Look again. Can it be? Write.

The last word shall go to my dear mother. Take heed all
communards of her pearls of wisdom. Who knows from what
depths of depravity her words may save you. 'I hope you will
soon feel the desire to put your talents and education to some

job which will stretch your mind so that the job demands so
much of your energies that you forget self.' "

My Tale, by Cathal Paddy Black for all ye English folks

"I left Dublin at ten in the morning by 'bus. The 'bus kept
stopping about every quarter of the hour, to collect eggs and
papers and things for people on the route to Donegal – it annoyed
me no end. I kept muttering abuses at the stupid red-neck of a
'bus driver for bein' so slow – eejit and what a fucken country
and so on.

It made no difference though, as the pattern continued – in fact
grew worse and more frequent coming towards Sligo. I was livid.

I never got to Burtonport that day – went in fact more towards
the North. Got drunk in a place called Raphoe – only had to buy
one drink, the rest the locals bought. 'Dublin Boy' they called
me if ye please; then they continued talking among themselves,
asking me every now and then was I all right. *I was fine.*

Slept the night in a Garda station in Lifford, freezing cold,
too much drink, rats and snakes in me bed. Ousted out at six
the next morning, pitch dark, footing me way to Letterkenny.
Arrived via tractor and 'bus and shoe leather in Atlantis at four
in the evening. Jenny and Oisin seemed really surprised. Oisin
looked like he was tripping, really changed since I'd seen him
last, really alive.

The first week or so, I felt I had to have a therapy session at
least once a day even if there was nothing there for Chrissake!
But slowly, I've been feeling my way into the place and the
people and I've been happier than I've ever been. Sometimes
it feels like when you walk up a hill and suddenly, when you
reach the top, the land lies before you beautiful and peaceful and
full, when you feel suddenly and beautifully lost – blessed, like
sudden rain on a close day. Anyway, that's the way I feel, like
I've come home after being away for so long.

I feel eternally grateful to you, Jenny.

love, Cathal."

Paul's Tale (aged 10)

"I'm Paul. I live in a therapeutic community. I've been in a therapeutic community for three years, nearly four years. I'm nearly eleven. I can easily annoy people and I suck my thumb.

In these nearly four years, I've moved to millions of places. Let me see. I've lived in Cumberland. Beautiful. I lived in a squat; it was all right. Then in fantastic Ireland. Then the bad bit, I went to school. Corporal punishment. Yuk.

Never mind, I got a girlfriend and now I play kiss chase every so often.

Love to everyone, Paul, x x x."

From a Visitor

"Atlantis
    House of Hope
        for many hurt people.

Andy came
    Cried a little
        Growled a bit more
            Roared a lot

Read a little
    Talked a bit more
        Thought a lot

Inishfree
    Just that
        Space to be

Andy left
    No 'terapy'
        but something more :
            Clear vision of a lifestyle
                Not seen or felt before.

Thanks for having me, love, Andy."

28th October, 1975
First Year Review of Atlantis

"A year now since we bought Atlantis. A year of comings and goings, of drunks knocking on the door after midnight asking for Terapy or Lettuces, but wanting women, of neighbours gradually tuning in, of bored and boring hitchers calling, of local acclaim for my house-size mural instead of the pitchforks, lynching and burning at the stake I'd phantasized; a year of goats, fences, then more goats and more fences; of chasing goats and mending fences, of goats in the kitchen and goats in the hall, goats up the stairway and me up the wall; a year of anxiety in the morning about starving goats and relief in the afternoon to see fat goats; a year of nasturtian-crazy, ballet-dancing silhouetted goats on rocks and of randy smelly Billy goat that cries like a wounded drunk in the night.

And the human inmates of Atlantis? Well, of course, Gino is the Chief Legendary Figure of the Risen City. In our dull moments, we gaze wistfully at the empty space in front of the range where once the Great Grotti warmed his regal bum and gazed blankly into Space. How me miss his burnt pans and the familiar scorched odour of his never-washed, never-changed, one-and-only Italian-style pyjama top, and the fetching sight of his famous Bum as seen through the ever-widening split in his one pair of Italian-style trousers. Who now will invite perfect strangers, male, female and indifferent, beautiful and ugly alike, fat and thin, old and young, to share his sensuous sweat-drenched sheets? Who now can match his boundless sparkling energy? Oh Gino, come back, we plead, to us! We will bring you peat to warm your bum, maidens to warm your tum, antibiotics to expel your mum, trumpets to block out the boredom of your days and alcohol to blot out the emptiness of your nights! Come! do not deprive us for too many moons of your mimes and antics, your cosmic wisdom, water-pistol fights, your jokes and your love of humanity and humwomanty alike. Grots may come and grots may go, but the memory of the grottiest guru of them all lingers on forever, along with the smell of the dirty socks you left me in the washing room.

Meanwhile, brown as a berry and amazingly merry in spite of labouring under the depressive influence of screwed-up parents, back sailed Rebecca to town, to join the Water Pistol Brigade, fall in love with Burtonport's chief thirteen-year-old ladykiller in tartan pants, and to cause to sicken with unsatisfied desire the otherwise unmeltable Frank the Mechanical Clank, Doughty Desperate Don, St. Anthony the Ever-Erect and of course, our own dear Gastronomical Grotti. But, spurning all advances, Rebecca herself pined away in secret sorrow, for the only Atlantean who could touch her girlish heart was an Australian Fence-Post called John.

Now this Australian was very good at putting up fences, but, unlike his brother Capricorns, he never learnt to jump over them. Farewell John, and may you live to build many more walls, until you are tired of them, when you might decide to devote your talents instead to knocking them down.

And now to our Ian, Defender of the Meek, and Chief Political Correspondent to the local newspaper; he is unequalled when it comes to Counteracting Capitalists in the Kitchen, chucking gravel stones at insurance hawkers, and pointing out the finer features of Glaswegian street-gang fighting to our Irish members. Lurking palely in Piscean waters, his galloping Aries Ascendant occasionally goads him out of bed to produce priceless pearls of wit and wisdom.

Around this time, with a hop, skip and a jump, there appeared on our front lawn armed with a pair of garden shears and conducting an invisible choir, Bernard the reluctant Heterosexual, singing at the top of his lungs all four parts of some obscure opera whilst whistling simultaneously the Irish Jig we heard played three thousand times at the Buncrana Folk Festival. Our handsome grasschopper has the habit of appearing and disappearing with disconcerting staccato effect: up a ladder touching up the imperfections of previous painters, hopping on hands and knees along gravel pathways waging a wondrous though

quite pointless war on weeds, swaying back and forth to some
Mozart melody whilst sawing a piece of wood, then popping off
one dark and thoughtful night to reappear through the letter-
box, announcing change of residence.

Now Frank, oft described, though hotly denied, as Man On
The Brink Having a Think, or Man Without Chink Unblocking
the Sink, or Man Without Kink Refusing a Drink, or Man
Chained in Clink Loosens a Link, he too has arrived and
departed, reappeared and redisappeared. Francis glances,
prances and advances. Sagittarius Frank, the Wooden Horse of
Try, try, try again: if the Primal Therapy don't splinter you,
then the Dynamic Meditation might. But our Frank's so keen
on struggling, he leaves no time for cuddling.

One of our first Irish arrivals was a Priestly Person by the
name of Saint Anthony. Having spent his growing years training
to be a Christian Brother, he arrived at the Gateway to Hell pale
with fear and four feet four, protesting extreme superiority and
total relaxation, but unable to open the door. Dear Saint
Anthony, who ran two hundred miles at the sight of his own
irrepressible erection, passion-flower Tony professing purity
whilst laying out married ladies in the long grass. Regaining his
self-composure somewhat through transcendental medication,
he returned to test anew his restored defences, but alas, all he
discovered was a note from the Court Bardess saying:

> Humpy Dumpy sat tight on his wall
> Trained and straining never to fall
> But nine months of tampering from our lady Jen
> Made sure he never held together again."

★ ★ ★

Yes, 1975 was the Springtime of Atlantis, Co. Donegal. When
I look back, four years later, on that first year, I see: naivety –
a great quality I reckon in this sophisticated, super-cynical
world – freshness, exuberance, enthusiasm. I think that's what
carried us through: after all, we were doing something mighty

strange: dumping a multi-coloured, outlandish, foreign culture
(foreign to *any* country!) on the doorstep of a quiet, super-
conventional Catholic Irish fishing and farming village, without
announcement, without so much as a by-your-leave, without
explanation, without a single solitary attempt to intermingle,
socialize or compromise. We landed from outer space, and we
quickly took root. And we were there for eighteen months before
anyone started making a fuss.

I don't really know what the locals thought of us – I think I
was too shy to find out. We didn't deliberately fraternize, but
just took our contact as it naturally happened: buying live yeast
from the local bakery; finding out how to cut turf and getting
shown the way to our turf bog; buying goats; letting neighbours
use the 'phone; repelling after-midnight drunks; going to the
occasional dance. I do remember being somewhat surprised that
young people locally didn't use the house more, for we were
open to all. I know if something like Atlantis had sprung up in
my home-town when I was a bored and frustrated and rebellious
teenager, I'd have leapt at the opportunity to break out of the
constraints of my background and I'd have fought my mother
viciously if she tried to stop me going. But then, in 1975, fresh
from England, I was only just learning about the intense
paranoia of the Catholic family system, with its invisible strangle-
hold on each person's private life, behaviour and movement.
Only the little children dared slip round the taboos, coming in
our back door, over our garden wall, playing truant from school
to come and play with our kids, in spite of admonishings from
the local priest that all good Burtonportian parents would main-
tain apartheid with Atlantean offspring. But as the years went
by, these kids too would gradually succumb to the psychological
mafia system as they became awkward, sexually awake and pain-
fully social-pressure-conscious teenagers. It took me a while to
understand exactly what the great Taboo was made of. Was it
really Religion? Culture Gap? Fear of the Unknown? I pon-
dered, amused, the echoes fed back to us that Atlantis was a
'brothel,' a particularly amazing hallucination during this first

year when often I was the only woman at Atlantis, and would have been mighty pleased had some lusty local crossed my threshold and claimed me. No such luck!

Now it all seems so simple: Sex is the answer. Sex is the great Catholic hunger, the great Mysterious NO; the major corrosive factor undermining the Church's supremacy. We hit where it hurt, and we didn't have to do anything at all. Just the hint of Difference – and I must say Atlantis did of course provide more than just a hint of difference! – and everyone's longings and fears were projected in black, white and high colour on to our community. What could we possibly be doing all day – not to mention all night – long, except what they wanted to do and were forbidden from doing? So what to us Englishers was just an organic part of planting cabbages, papering walls, sorting out headaches and discovering that Irish food-prices were double those in London, became ALL that we did (apart from taking drugs of course, because everyone knows that women with long skirts and men with beards take drugs). I was astonished; for even I, who just about dared to paint those astrological signs all over my house, would never have had the gall to set up a brothel on Burtonport high street!

And so to therapy: When I started offering 'primal therapy' at Atlantis, I had this grand idea that anyone coming to sort themselves out would live outside the commune to start with, maybe in a Bed & Breakfast place or Youth Hostel, and not mingle with us on a day-to-day living basis. That way I thought to keep people's madness, heavy demands and neurotic trips from getting tangled up in our hair, sleep, jam and toothpaste. Some chance! I was never cut out to be a super-cool, objective, white-coated therapist. There was no way I could keep people that annoyed me out of my kitchen, or people that I loved out of my heart. Oh, I tried it for a while, the B&B bit, but very soon I slipped back into the irresistability of Being Human, throwing everyone in at the deep end, myself included, and seeing what came out of it. What came of it for me was that I had to define my boundaries on the spot, more and more: to learn to say, 'no, NO, and *NO*!' And I had to wrestle with guilt: Was it legitimate for someone I'd promised therapy to, to knock on my bedroom door at eight o'clock in the morning and vibe me that if he didn't have a session immediately, he'd die – or more likely, I would (he being 6ft. 3in.)? (No). Was sorting out someone's life-mess more important than getting a sun-tan? (No). Did I owe someone, who had paid me £200, more attention than someone who'd borrowed tuppence from me? (No). And especially, Did I have to love people I hated? (NO). Also, did I have to put up with burnt veg. or an overdose of curry powder in the food just because the day's cook wasn't in touch with their aggression? (*NO!*). And finally, was it all right to hate someone on sight and know that no amount of Therapy would ever make them a loveable human being? (YES).

What was Atlantis like, organized – or unorganized – in this fashion, for the average (no such thing) therapy-seeker? Guessing: a relief for those wanting contact and human warmth and 'ordinariness' – a very unusual quality Out There; an irritation to those seeking Structure, Their Rights, or the Proper Way; a frightening place – for everyone at times – and especially for those who found it most difficult to 'go with the flow', to let things happen, to ask for and push for what they needed; and an exciting place always for everyone. No two days could ever be the same; you never knew what would happen next, who would walk in or who would walk out. And this is the only aspect of Atlantis which has remained constant throughout the years – its unpredictability.

And so to Year Two . . .

1976

ATLANTIS YEAR TWO: SUMMER

Just like to tell you something
Don't want to lay down the law
But I'd like to save you from the false temples
That stand on the Valium Shore.

Despair is a dark valley that leads you
To the lair of the Minotaur
But there's no Ariadne to lead you through
And no thread goes before.
You go sliding down the slipway
And the sign says: 'Last Exit to Hope.
And the Problems pile up like confetti
As you hide behind your last stash of dope.
You're locked in a sightless prison
And the bars are of your own device
You're surrounded by the death of your past
And your head's in a self-closed vice.
And your fantasies stand like cold sentinels
Like ghosts on the edge of the Moon.
Oh, you child of the favoured West,
There's cancer in your silver spoon.

That's when you visit the false temples
That stand on the Valium Shore,
And the white-coated whore
Who soothes like your daddy
Just offers you one pill more.
'You're mad and you're sad
And you're probably bad,
So just swallow me one pill more.'

You sit a sad prisoner in the cells of help
And shit silts in through your pores,
And the net result is you run the risk
Of swapping their madness for yours.
You must know your head is your own
And no-one can take it away;

You must know you're alive in your very own body
And you must remember you're there to stay.

But while you live in the false temples
That stand on the Valium Shore,
That white-coated whore
Who soothes like your daddy,
Will offer you one pill more.
'This world is empty with no sweet honey
Sweat for your sins and sweat for your money
So just adjust to the money store,
And swallow me one pill more.'

Your daddy's dead and you're in your head
And you are in control,
Push through the trouble, heave aside the rubble
And mine for the gold in your soul.
Now is the time to count your coins
And reckon your own true worth
For the safe that holds the cashier's pen,
Is guarded by the Children of Earth.

Here there are no temples
And we do not presume
To know you or to weigh you
We only give you room.

The Valium Shore
by Jeremy Ward

★   ★   ★

1976, 'SUMMER' of Atlantis: a flowering, maturing, ripening, expanding. We are getting better and better known; our London commune is very big, often thirty or more people; Atlantis House in Ireland is always full; people clamouring to come for therapy; we say 'yes' to them all. I feel more political about what we are doing: everyone's family background is part of society; sorting out personal hangups becomes a political act if you go through with it whole-heartedly. Facing parents, partners and friends with our inner truth sometimes becomes a major event involving neighbours, police action, court injunctions, newspaper scandal campaigns, bizarre accusations. Atlantis becomes notorious, and 'all' we are doing is getting to know ourselves and one another and starting to tell friends and relations what we really feel and think. That shakes them up, and accusations fly: we are 'brainwashing', 'changing people's personalities', 'deliberately breaking up families.' Heavy political methods are brought in to stop personal expression: the personal *is* the political. Things that happen in every kitchen, bedroom and bathroom throughout the land, when aired and talked about honestly, cause the uneasy equilibrium of patched-up nuclear family life to tip, topple and crumble. All fingers point to Atlantis: we are to blame! It's obvious, we rocked the boat. Why, if we hadn't, perhaps no-one would have noticed the boat was on the rocks anyhow. Atlanteans living their lives militantly, not being content to suffer their pains in silence, and all hell is set loose – coming in our direction. Amazing.

20th January, 1976
Dream

I am in an old disused house at the bottom of my mother's garden.

There is a fuzzy light sensation as if something is working itself up ready to explode and I move quickly right out of the door just as the whole building goes up in flames. The whole lower garden catches fire and there is a narrow strip of fire travelling as fast as I am up the garden. I call to my mother to get the fire brigade and meanwhile I look frantically for something to beat out the edge of the flames. My mother is dreamily pottering around the garden with no sense of urgency.

Shrieking and screaming and flapping up the garden towards me are dozens of little chicken-like creatures who want me to save them. Some are really tiny, no bigger than moths, all flapping around helplessly, totally vulnerable and completely dependent on my will to save them. I have to touch them really delicately so as not to damage them. Amongst them also are some old cocks which are limping through having had to walk and run so far; they are flapping and squawking in complaint. I pick up one of the tiny chick creatures and it nuzzles into the palm of my hand in tremendous relief. I have it in mind to go back and save the rest, but it all seems such a wearisome task, and I am in almost as much a haze as my mother.

26th February, 1976
To a German boyfriend of ten years ago
"Dear Volkhard,

Your image of yourself as a rational man and of me as a nutty woman are both completely wrong. Anyone who kids himself up he's being objective has lost touch altogether! Even those who devote their lives to becoming machines don't manage it. I trust only those who declare, express and enjoy their prejudices! I am prejudiced against Virgos (you), women's libbers, nasty rational left-wing political groups and all big-headed, small-hearted, fight-the-invisible-enemy-but-don't-make-a-personal-fuss type movements. I am prejudiced in favour of lively energetic unspoilt crazy people who don't try and rationalize their craziness.

You ask what I've been doing since the end of my story in *Room To Breathe* – since summer 1973. Well, I've been leading a revolution, Volkhard, the same revolution I've been working for since the age of seventeen and longing for since the age of eight when first I began to emerge from the fog. The revolution I am engaged in is the one I was sensing myself towards at the time of heartbreak over Vicky's suicide in 1966. Vicky for me symbolizes the total failure of the left-wing intellectual scene; my own near-suicide I translated into energy to fight, not capitalistic phantoms, but my mother and father inside me, the shitty parts of all my relatives and friends, the violence in myself towards my own child, the stuck anger and terror in her of me. I have turned my own deathliness into fighting sickness wherever I find it. I don't put down my 'political' days, my involvement in the anti-nuclear weapons movement; I feel that what I am doing now is a continuation of that, is in fact even more political. Atlantis is a spearhead, a campaign which alters forever at root every person who stays here: no-one who works on themselves here for any length of time leaves a manipulable person; no-one can ever get on top of you again if you fully find yourself – they'd have to physically kill you first. Everyone who lives at Atlantis gains the basic confidence which is knowing yourself, knowing what you want, what you feel and think; everyone who stays here works towards developing their maximum effectiveness as a human being. Your average politico does all sorts of terrible things to himself, to his kids, to his friends and lovers whilst busily working towards a 'better future.' What we are doing here is bringing that better future right into the present. There is nothing so convincing as a happy revolutionary! Who in their right senses would want to buy the philosophical goods offered by the miserable, tight, rigid, fucked-up people you know and I know who fill the ranks of so many left-wing organizations?

I am absolutely determined that Atlantis should be the centre of a cosmic campaign to change the direction of the world, not a rest-home for retired neurotics!

Jen."

7th March, 1976
"Dear Alex,

Atlantis come to a dead stop because I've moved to live out here on Inishfree Island? You must be joking! I had expected a certain amount of emotional constipation because of the overwhelming percentage of new people, but none such. Those who have been here five weeks are terribly fierce with those who've been here five days, and people get thrown into the deep end straight away. The groups are high energy, long and frequent.

Sometimes Babs and I do very little work at all: I give practically no sessions and Babs gives a minimal amount considering she has technically about half a dozen 'intensives' going. They get their intensives all right, more intense than ever before, and people shift faster, but an intensive might consist of getting told you can't have any more sessions with Babs and having an intense period of getting into feelings about that with someone else. It works wonders, an excellent system, especially as no-one invented it. But just in case you run away with any big ideas about an easy life, Alex, let me say you will on no account be allowed to share this system when you join us, as your own intensive will be to have to care for people sacredly, diligently, and lovingly, for the whole of their growth, with Babs and me standing over you with a hatchet watching how you behave. So much as a hint of a snarl from you and . . .! Our system works only for those of us who are basically overly-kindly, loving, caring, conscientious, generous people, not for mean Scottish hard-nuts like you!

Dearest love, how well we will harmonize when you come hither.

Meanwhile, both you and Becky's father have written worrying about there being 'No Room at the Inn' here for you. O men of little faith! Do you not know that I am not fickle, and my oldest friends (provided they are clean-living and have no emotional arrears with me) are ever closest to my heart (even if I can't stand their character-structures) (or their eating habits), and how could you think I would ditch you for new flames in my life (quite easily)?

Seriously though, sweetheart, your claim to a place in Atlantis is built upon the solid rock of years of conflict with Yours Truly, JJ."

Inishfree, 14th April, 1976
"To Clive, on hearing he'd taken an overdose

Well, when in this mood that I am in, I can quite well feel how if any of us could see what lies ahead in therapy, none of

us would start, a bit like life really, so it's just as well we don't
see, or we could all drop into the sea together right away and
save the agony. I don't know if your troubles are in the present,
mine aren't, as I have quite the most amazing bloke I could
have dreamed up, and some pretty good fellow-communards,
and a little bit of paradise scooped up and saved from the cars,
for how long I don't know. My sadness lies in being a fatherless
child, and it truly is very difficult to fill an emptiness that big,
and with you there must be very little to hold on to for your
barrenness in the children's home was more complete. It will get
worse the more you feel, there are no two ways about it. It will
definitely get worse and worse. Your angers will get worse and
your wants will get bigger and your needs will get more hateful,
and your resentments will grow into twenty-feet-high walls
around you, and all the warmth and colour in the world will just
make you want to die. That's how it is. The alternatives are
simple: 200 aspirins taken efficiently in secret; holding everything in and staying biologically alive whilst going mad in your
head; or suffering a little more publicly and sharing your feelings.
I am not very good at the latter way myself. I get secretive and
paranoid when I am down. I don't want even my lover to know;
he wouldn't want me then I think, if he knew how ugly I feel,
and how I am worried about my age and if he knew how when
I look at him, I feel he is too beautiful and too alive for me,
and I'm a gonner and therapy doesn't work and what's the point,
and my daughter is a wreck and can't express herself and here's
Oisin wanting a new baby out of my guilt-ridden body.

What is amazing is how narrow the gap is between living and
dying. It's like cursing and swearing with the wind blowing from
behind you so that your hair gets in your eyes and nose and
teeth and you can't see what you're doing, then if you swivel
around in anger, miraculously your face is blown fresh and clean
and you can see perfectly; it might take your breath away for a
second and cut rather sharply into your skin, but the difference
is amazing.

Now I can go for two or even three days gritting my teeth and tensing my muscles and not getting a session because I've forgotten about Hope; but then my dreams take over and the pains get so bad, there's just no point; I'm sure I'm dead, but then I lie down with a friend listening, and it really is extraordinary how bodies work by themselves. As far as I know, this is all that therapy can give : a low tolerance level for pain and tension, so that you have to expel the cause of it. It doesn't really matter what methods you use to come alive, though I would have thought aspirins were pretty sickening to swallow, not to mention a bit boring putting all those nasty-tasting globules mechanically one by one or two by two into your mouth, but I guess it would work as well as therapy if the goal is relief from pain.

But in times like these, though my memory is dimmed, I do in fact recall that sudden three-dimensionalness when colour comes seeping through and a good session has suddenly switched the balance between hope and death. I am not in that now, but I do remember, just about, the feel of warm sun on my skin, and the sudden flood in my body when I find that sexuality is a possession of my very own and not something over there to be sought after and worked for. My head is aching, but I do remember, and I lean back and trust, out of habit now, that the tide will turn. It isn't easy, the damage seems so basic and total: how can I conjure up a long-legged daddy to rush down the garden after and chatter to, when in fact he was just a shadow in my brain, and there never was a garden, and my chattering has long since died inside me? Yet there is my need: I still want to run around after this tall figure who will show me the world, introduce me to the mechanics of living and fight off all marauding outsiders who might try to come into my life before I am ready. It didn't happen, I am 34, and the deathliness lies heavy in my fingers as I write to you.

The blank corridors and lined up beds and rows of toilets and timed dinner-hours, the desolate totality and unendingness of a children's home where you have no hint as yet that this is not the sum total of the universe, will take nothing less than all the hatred and bitterness put into you to reverse. You will have to harness yourself to a revolutionary cart of Hatred: there is no carrot, and no reward. It's no good thinking you'll get the goodies in the end, because you won't; there is absolutely nothing to look forward to, and if you do, you'll be disappointed. If the task of eradication of your chains is itself not stimulating and rewarding enough for you, then you might as well give up. Therapy is not a means to an end, it is the only way to live that presents itself to those of us who have not been satisfied with birthday cakes, shop windows and good marks. I can't really think of anything constructive that you can do with your misery, except make a terrible nuisance of yourself to all your friends in the most creative way possible. I guess if you lie down in the corridor and kick and yell when everyone has just gone to bed, or start butting into people if you feel ignored, you might call forth some kind of response. It's not the best kind of contact, but you never know where it might lead, and it's more exciting and much healthier than a cool aspirinic death.

The goats are coming over the hill and milking time is nigh. The chicks have stopped beeping and are huddled together; they think it's night-time. But there's still a load of yelling to be done in here tonight. I've just seen Billy goat leaping madly sideways off the rocks; they come home in a different mood each night do the goats. Last night it was Everyone on to Sara, biting and butting her till she ran off into the rain. Well, I don't know whether a week-old goat kid, a mad fighting cock, twenty-seven rushing flapping balls of yellow fluff and a lot of new friends would do you any good, but Inishfree is a people-sized world and there's turf to be cut and seeds to be sown and rainy days round the fire weaving dreams of water-tanks and bath-houses. I know we're not friends, but when London palls, Ireland pulls, and it's difficult to think of suicide when you've got hold of a roll of barbed wire while Oisin bangs the staples in. Try it.

Jen."

Letter to a Patient
25th April, 1976
"Dear Helen,

It is obviously right for you to have left Atlantis, just as we urged you to do. Here you started to see the problems; you got a taste of a different way of relating. And now your uphill climb really begins. You have an enormous journey ahead of you. You are on an impossible quest to find the Crack of Doom and destroy the Ring, destroy the Chain that is destroying you (and the rest of the world, but that is a problem for later). Yours is no easy task; I knew that the first time I worked with you. Your aura is so diffuse, so confused and blurred with the shadows and ghosts of other people trying to live in you and through you and for you, that I could hardly see a way for you to win through. But I am a messianic madwoman and I know that if you look too carefully at the task ahead, reason and common sense will tell me and you not to attempt to climb up the mountain. It's only when you face each boulder and bramble patch as it comes that there is any chance at all of making your way through the impassable. Fools rush in where angels fear to tread, but fools have more fun than angels, and I'm afraid it's only mad fools that have a chance of sorting out the 6,000-year-old mess we've inherited.

When you talk about the 'little part of you that doubts you'll ever get what you want out of therapy', you are in fact talking about the huge part of you that doubts whether you'll ever get what you want full stop. I would have thought you'd been here long enough to know that there is no such thing as therapy. Therapy doesn't exist as some entity separate from you and me. All the word can mean is the healing forces within you which, combined with the life-force inside me and your other life-positive friends, can help you redefine your damaged boundaries and rekindle your childhood honesty and your capacity to love realness in people instead of settling for sugar-icing. Your best therapist will turn out to be your little sister and your best session will occur the day you suddenly and clearly know what you want, and go out straight and get it, without reference to me or any other mummy or daddy figure.

As long as you keep swimming in your confusion without giving up or dying, the toy penguin you carry around with you will turn into a fairy prince, though he won't look anything at all like you imagined, and you may have a devil of a job recognizing him at first. Where you're at, practically anyone you choose to fix your affections on will be disastrous, as you've obviously not yet climbed down on the side of the fence called 'taking your life into your own hands', but are still stuck up there looking longingly at the sugar-icing your family would just love to provide you with.

Helen, look, I know some magic. You have to do just two things: stay breathing and keep writing to me whenever you need to. Use me as a goddess like I had to use my therapist as god for a while. It works like this: you write your triumphs and despairs on paper to me. You then get no feedback from me for at least a week because of the postal service. Hence you will have reached out in desperation or elation to a real human being who is prevented by time and space from doing anything at all for you in the moment. This is exactly what you need. By the time you get my reply, you will have had to sort out whatever-it-was for yourself or rejoice alone, and my words will come to you simply as a bolster to give you the strength to carry on up the next bit of the mountain. Obviously, the whole difficult process can be curtailed by suicide, which will solve all your problems forever and save you a lot of work and headaches. This is where you have to become a crusader, for there will be no dividends in the present as long as you are looking for them. Sugar-icing melts in the hand into a sticky mess. Your greatest joy will come the day you suddenly realize you just waded through a smelly and dangerous swamp all on your own and were so intent upon getting through it, so absorbed in your task, that you didn't stop to bemoan your fate or get sucked under.

You have come to therapy with perhaps the biggest handicaps of anyone else this past year. The law of Karma says something

like the heavier the knapsack you carry, the greater your triumph
when you get to the top of the mountain. I know that's not much
comfort when you feel so weighted down, you can't look up at
the sun.

Don't try to understand this letter, or anything Alex or me or
anyone tells you. We're all terribly wise, but it's you who has
to stand naked in front of a full-length mirror and breathe very
deeply and let yourself know who you are."

'SUNDAY INDEPENDENT', May 30th, 1976
" 'I'D PREFER ATLANTIS TO THE MEN IN WHITE
COATS!', Says Patrick Murray

In Burtonport, Co. Donegal, among the white-washed cottages
and neatly painted houses, stands Atlantis. Painted all colours
of the rainbow, with great red eyes over its windows, Atlantis
is an imposing sight in the Donegal fishing town.

Inside its multi-coloured doors, Jenny James tries to make
people happy. All of the two dozen people in Atlantis have been
or are depressed. All have a need for company, a need to talk
about their experiences, and most of all, a need to unwind.

Jenny and her guests do not believe in psychiatrists. The
system they use in Atlantis is known as Primal Therapy. Primal
therapy encourages those who feel they have something bottled
up inside them to let it out. Feelings of anger against parents,
teachers, or whatever, are released.

The person undergoing the therapy hits out at cushions, often
screaming and shouting. This releases feelings which have remained hidden for years. 'People who have emotional problems
often find that it stems from treatment they received as a child
at the hands of parents or teachers. This feeling of hate . . .
never leaves them. Friends, children, often suffer as a result,'
Jenny explained.

. . . Emotional release therapy 'cleans' the subject. They leave Atlantis, or its sister commune in London, with new confidence and self-determination.

They come to Atlantis from all over the world. During our visit there, we met Dubliners, Londoners, Glaswegians, an Australian. There have been Swedes and other Scandinavians there.

The commune has now bought two houses on Inishfree Island. 'It is really growing,' Jenny said.

Locals in Burtonport were suspicious at first. Some thought it was a 'nut house', others thought it was a brothel. But now with one or two exceptions, the visitors to Atlantis get on well with the locals."

In September 1976, because of a breakdown in a love affair that was very important to me, I felt I needed to go away from Atlantis for a while myself, to feel out who I was Out There once more, after my incredibly intense emotional life in the commune. I wanted to see how I would cope, how I would relate to the people I chanced to meet, what I would feel like, how I would view what I saw around me. It was counsel I often gave to others, and now I took it for myself.

I was lucky in having a strong woman, Jill, to take care of things while I was away, and a good solid thriving community to keep my home warm for me to return to – no, not lucky, I'd earnt it!

8th September, 1976
"Hello Jill,

My high-heeled shoes held me up well on the road to Dublin. I was a London girl feeling younger with every step as my newly-hennaed tarted-up hair fluffed around me and my city clothes gave me that go and get feeling, don't sit around and wait.

I was in love with September Ireland like an unbelievable TWO years ago when on a September road I found Atlantis. The hot air, full moon and still waters were the same, just a different pair of shoes and now a different direction – back to the city grime, and I knew that in no place on this journey would we pass through such peace and beauty as in Co. Donegal, in spite of the baked bean cans and crisp packets occasionally decorating the heather.

Alan and I walked many miles until a driver who knew you, Jill, picked us up and we talked about Atlantis therapy, and then the hurdy-gurdy started: a pub crawl no less! Our driver insisted. A good experience once, though I wouldn't want to repeat it too often. The pub owner at Fintown was busy replacing a broken toilet mirror. 'Someone put his fist through the last one.' he said. 'I don't know what they get out of it,' he said. 'Releasing tension', said his wife. 'They'd be better to scream.' 'And it's cheaper,' said he.

I relaxed purring on my high chair, feeling at home in spite of the plastic decorations. The men started talking about sheep maggots and I felt embarrassed to be so involved and in tune with them, being a sheep-keeper myself. I wondered a little if my city friend, Alan, sitting silently to my left, might not resent my at-homeness, but he said he didn't, and so I got very involved with sheep maggots indeed, and know now how to detect and cure them (run the sheep under a cold tap), which is most important I was warned, because Lambs Can Drop Dead in Two Days from them.

And so to the next pub – a halfway stop, the man explained; halfway that is, between the last mile and the next mile. And here Ireland came right into my veins, not just the cider, but old ladies singing, 'Danny Boy', and I felt so moved I went and congratulated them on their singing. They had confetti in their hair and button-hole carnations, but no bride to be seen: off attempting to accommodate the man she's always been taught to keep out I guess.

I could feel this country from the inside for a while: the pub is their encounter group and there is a high degree of love and honesty exchanged, an intimate relating to strangers with drink the passport, an expensive, damaging and repetitive therapy certainly, but still their faces were aglow with a robustness and liveliness that warmed me to them and I felt harmonious with their ways of relating for a while.

The Gaelic for 'Yes' seems to be 'No', so I was given more drinks than ever in my life before. I felt absolutely marvellous – until we found ourselves getting into a van with a thoroughly drunken driver and I was terrified. Alan shared my concern, and we got out of the van after a heart-stopping few miles and landed ourselves on a country road in the middle of the night, which was better than in the graveyard anyway.

Kisses to all the sweet illusioned communards of that castle in the fresh air to which I shall one day return. More news from the Outside soon.

love, Jen."

"Dear Maurice,

Here I sit pained and strained at midnight on a hard bed-base with a stinky sleeping-bag around me, a Dublin Street just feet away through uncurtained windows and the stench of new and expensive and ugly paint in my already-stinging nose, my daughter asleep beside me.

Yes, I have arrived in the Great Outside World, and the most wonderful part of it all, for you my dear, is that I feel like shit. Now you may rejoice! Raise your voice and sing praises to your own personal devil, for the woman who so wronged you by leaving your manly side is feeling *dreadful*. I have encountered nothing but illness in this great outside. 'Well, what did you expect . . .' I know, I know, too true, but here it is, unfaceably staring me in the face in the form of the WALLPAPER these terribly 'alternative' people have put on their alternative walls, and the alternative STINK of this christianly lent sleeping-bag and no mattress and no soya sauce in the kitchen and no beautiful man to sleep with ('I should hope not' – OK, OK), and worst of all, here we have my girlfriend's 26-year-old bloke getting up early in the morning in order to creep home to daddy's house so that daddy won't notice he's been away living his own life, and 25-year-old Paul saying to me 'why don't you creep in when my mother's asleep, she'll be gone in the morning and won't notice you.' Thanks a lot, says I, and what if we should happen to meet on the way to the toilet in the middle of the night? So off he goes home alone to this great big house and he thinks of me and he wishes to be free, but he cannot see, no he cannot see (thank you Dory Previn).

What am I doing, you may well ask, in Dublin's grey city where the folk are so shitty and when I know that my true love is my own dear sweet home? Well, I'm not so sure, and if I don't find out, I'll be straight back. I'm afraid I can't send you love, I'm in no mood to; I've got cold feet and even more than a man to cuddle, I'd like a decent bed tonight.

Jen."

"Hello Maurice,

Oh my god plastic roses everywhere round the mirror, in the hall, on the table, up the walls, non-Catholic parents who just happened to send him to communion and who have Italian saint magazines polluting the kitchen table, and then there's his non-Catholic sister who goes to Mass 'because the kids have started school.' Oh the sickness, the deadness, the suffocating hygiene, the blocked-up fireplaces displaying artificial logfires run on electricity, the windows barred up, not a stir of air in the house. Sterility rules, while he pins a poster on the wall saying, 'If you've stopped being born, you've started to die'; Reich and Laing in his bookcases and books on the sexuality he's hardly sampled; and hate and contempt in his voice as he shows me round his mother's house which is 'too comfortable to leave.'

I slept in his dead father's bed with Becky, a night of disturbed thoughts, all raging around the subject of Catholicism. I had never realized just how much of a social rat-race Catholicism is;

somehow I had always believed it was an emotional, mystical, passionate religion for the needy, the gullible, the miserable, the soft-at-heart. I didn't know before that they go to Mass as a status symbol, to keep their jobs, and that they thrash their kids and teach them the evils of sexuality in order to keep up with the O'Joneses. Dublin is disgusting. In Donegal, Catholicism somehow seems more natural, more rooted amongst the gorse-bushes. Here it is just a disease. No free schools, not a single whisper or glimmer of a movement amongst 'radicals' to do anything about the church, the kids or their own barren lives. Yesterday I saw stuck on a bikinied woman in a drink advert, 'THIS ADVERTISEMENT IS INSULTING TO WOMEN'. So the women's libbers have made it to town. How totally irrelevant. They've copied, they're imports, plastic replicas from Britain and America superimposed on a situation where there's no personal freedom full stop, where people haven't even started to look at what's oppressing them, and when they do see, they usually leave the country, leave it to rot, because in Ireland, the social and the personal are one and the same thing: here the lefties can't kid themselves up that it's 'the system' they have to fight. Any move they would make would have immediate per-sonal repercussions and they'd have to face the fight where it really is: in their own parlour and kitchen and bedroom, with their own dear mummies and daddies and friends and relations and priests and schoolteachers. Absolutely no-one in Ireland dares do this; there'd be a revolution immediately. So they leave to fight a conveniently invisible enemy elsewhere and they come home for Christmas and the family weddings; or else they stay here, go blind, deaf, dumb and daft and hunt obscure issues to wax eloquent over their seventh pint of beer before going home alone to Their house, and to think of a future 'one day . . .' No wonder the lefties hate Atlantis and try to call *us* unpolitical!

I'm raging, yes, I'm raging about this country Maurice, the country of your parents which you dreamed of returning to. Well, now you're here I hope you'll do something about it when you've sorted yourself out, 'cos it certainly is, as my dad used

to sing, 'the most distressful country that man has ever seen.'
But at least it can be *seen,* that's the beauty of Ireland. The
issues are blatant, staring you in the face, not hazy and complicated by a thousand twisted strands of horror like in England.

All these words, impotence at midnight. I want to come back
to Donegal where we can get on with the job of training soldiers
to change the world. Out here, the Dreadful has undoubtedly
already happened. I suppose up there we can go on growing
grass for a few years yet, but I'll have to close my mind to all
these doomed babies being born, or I'll go mad.

I'm so unhappy here that at this moment I hate Ireland completely; the next time a lorry driver asks me 'and do you like it
here?' I'll say: 'the wind and the sea and the rocks and my
animals are just beautiful, and there was a time once when you
knew how to build fine cottages, but I just can't stand to see
what you are doing to yourselves and to your kids.' I'm going
to make war now wherever I go: I shall spit in the eye of every
left-winger, of everyone who counts himself radical, unless he is
actively loudly providing a living alternative to the Christian
Smotherers and their delightful version of hell on earth.

Well, I guess you don't feel I'm writing you a very personal
letter, but these are the matters my head is full of to the exclusion
of all else at the moment. I haven't made my mind up yet
whether to creep straight back home or whether to go for further
dosage to London; yesterday I was so down I couldn't bear the
thought of ploughing onward, but as Sue says, the first day is
always the worst, a bit like your first cigarette, after a while you
don't notice it's choking you to death.

                                    Till another day, Jen."

October 1976, Atlantis

"Friend Bernard,

Only twenty-four hours ago, I was boring myself to death in
a Dublin airport lounge, seeing Becky off to Germany, and now
here I am home again, with a life-time passed by in between,
sitting looking at the chickens being really silly outside my

window, doing all the things they've been taught that chickens do.

I was so glad to have on the 'phone a firm indication that you will be leaving London for here soon. It is time for an Exodus homeward! All fair Inishfreeans and Atlanteans have dallied too long in the regions of Mordor and may get permanently polluted if they don't wend their way back to the enchanted palace soon.

This morning as I cleaned the cooker, I experienced total ecstasy! I just knew there was nothing in the world I'd rather be doing than cleaning that cooker, for it was no ordinary cooker. Its meaning stretched outwards from me in all directions: this is my cooker in my home; I have a cooker to clean and a home to come back to. When I clean the cooker, I hear the voices of the people I live with and my ecstasy increases: these are the people I am living with and these are the people I want to live with. They came here for many strange reasons like thinking they are ill and wanting to be looked after or looking for enlightenment, all sorts of reasons, but the main thing is they are here and their jokes and laughter and talk about apple crumble is coming through to me and I am completely ecstatic. I have on a very short dress and I have had a bath and I feel my body slim and young and supple and I can feel every part of me. In Dublin, I felt Fat; there was only Food to be had in the city, the sexless city of Dublin, and that's why the people there get fat and flabby and smoke and wear make-up.

At my cooker, I just knew: I am living in paradise. It was definitely worth a pilgrimage to Dublin to feel this. I wasn't sure whether I'd come back to Maurice, the Scorpio man I left here, but he gave me such an unheld-back welcome on the 'phone and was so open and straightforward in his delight at me returning, that I find myself on the Other Side in this relationship: being wooed and holding back for obscure reasons of my own. There really isn't any point in this, so I have let him in by degrees and I think he may well have something to do with how I came to find ecstasy at the gas-cooker this morning. It really is true that all of us are all kinds of people within one lifetime: in my life,

I have breathed in cigarette smoke; in my life I have driven a car dangerously because I wanted to kill; in my life I have closed off and tried to vibrate people dead; in my early therapy days, I defended myself tightly against a whole group who were trying to probe into me – I was trying to stand up for the absoluteness of the Awful Position of women in society and rearing up fiercely when people kept asking me, 'what is the effect on you personally?' I didn't want to look at my own power and anger. And I have run a thousand miles over and over again to avoid feelings, and I have been a violently-withholding-violence pacifist and I have been a Headcase Intellectual; I have been a believer in the inevitable Progress of modern civilization; I have hated the countryside and I have wanted to see all the houses in one street uniformly painted the same colour; I have wanted to see the Fiction section in libraries done away with because only Facts matter; I believed at 'O' level that I knew everything there was in the world; I believed that it was wrong to pick up a child when it cries because 'it spoils them', and I have been in black pits waiting for a boyfriend to pick me up; I have sulked and pretended and hidden and laid trips and used intellectual wiles and emotional weapons, all to keep my pride and my stiffness of face; I have played every female game in the book; I have hated and criticized and played weak – I have been on all sides, I know the ins and outs of such positions well. So I am on the Other Side in this relationship, and I am viewing the world from yet another new angle today, and I feel fresh and in love with life.

Goodnight, love, Jen."

28th October, 1976   (Away from home again)
"Oisin,

I have just spent two hours of paranoia walking the housing estates looking for Mary. I can't find her, so now I have to wait for you in this pub and buy myself a drink for the first time in my life. My head is whirring, my ears ringing. I feel it really is too late, there is nothing we can do, it's too late for this world out here, all we can do is save ourselves. Everything I see makes me feel ghastly. How is it that I can be so paranoid in a country that is not mine, be oppressed by a religion that is not mine, feel so bowed down by a culture that is not mine, be cowed by a sexual morality which is, however, identical to that of Dartford, Kent, in the nineteen-fifties?

I need to be with you, but my thoughts are full of the times you have let me down. I feel deadened and numbed. I wish we hadn't split up to hitch here. I got a lift all right, in a Jaguar driven by a man who boasted his open-mindedness, sincerity and individuality. He was a Catholic with six children. He sent them to Mass. 'They like to go,' he explained.

I fell into a daze in that man's car. I was not honest or alive. I could not find a way to be myself. He was rich and self-satisfied and so delighted to have someone listen for two hours to his diluted philosophy of mediocrity and boredom.

The pub is filling up. I will try and dare to stay here till you turn up. I will do what everyone in Ireland does when they are paranoid. If it gets too bad, I will drink more till my surface tensions are obliterated.

I have seen you, Oisin, enslaved, sitting in this pub, and now I am enslaved. I am stunned with boredom, frozen with cold, weary of leg and mind. Every face I passed as I walked, I looked into. Every old woman was an anti-sexual enemy, even those who pleasantly told me the way. Everything looks so NORMAL in these Irish towns. The normality terrifies me. I remember years ago trying to help a man from Yugoslavia to come alive. He had been beaten up regularly as a child. It was normal in Yugoslavia he told me. It is normal in Ireland.

I see a little girl playing. She is perhaps like your sisters once were, before they became like nuns. I wonder to myself, how does anyone survive in this place? How could your brother have returned here after being away in England? Why do you keep returning? Even last month you returned here. I see nothing here but drabness and suffocation. I feel like lying down and dying rather than struggling to understand. All I know is, I cannot live out here. And yet, I too have returned. I have returned to you, Oisin, to all the torture of being with you. I too have returned to the safety of known pains.

I smell soup, but I do not dare to go and ask for soup. It may have killed animals in it I rationalize. I feel drunk after half a cider.

My thoughts about you are black. I cannot survive in this place for two hours without you, and yet you were here for five weeks, and before that for twenty-three years. I feel inadequate in the face of such endurance. You did not even masturbate you say; I cannot compete with such a fine record!

There is someone playing pool over there who sounds like Roy. I wish it was Roy. I cannot survive here, I cannot stay. I feel I am dying. Everyone else has died already. I am not very alive. I need so much to keep me going. I cannot support myself. I need my home. I am just like everyone else: I am paranoid of the rest of the world. I am just like my mother. She made a warm castle too, to invite people to. I think primal therapy is so much nonsense, and I am insane. I particularly think I am mad to put advertisements in magazines saying 'come and live with me in my house.' I think that is a very strange and unusual thing to do, a very weird way to communicate. We are reduced to very strange ways of expressing our needs.

I have just bought some soup. It was easy and it is made of vegetables. The peat fire is burning. Perhaps soon I will dare to sit in front of it.

The soup is out of a packet and cost seventeen pence."

Letter to a young Irish teacher
"Dear Mike,

To me it seems so obvious that we must break some mighty chains and reverse the karmic wheel unless we are to trudge on forever in mediocrity towards a grey death! However, I accept that this is not at all obvious to you, and that your own reservations and fears about confronting the Christian Brothers who have handled you so violently in the past are making you question Oisin's actions with his parents. I feel I am having to swim against great raging seas of different life experiences in order to reach you.

Ultimately, only getting in touch in a deep and powerful way with your own fury at what has been done to you can convince you of the need for reversal, for changing creatively, effectively and energetically the great balance of power which is always weighted against the more-alive and wielded by the deader elements in society. Most people who come to Atlantis think at first that there's nothing they can do to change things now, that they can never get what they didn't get, that there's no point in starting to be real with their parents who are 'getting old', who 'meant well'; 'why bother them?', 'let them die in peace,' 'it'll only give her a heart-attack' and so on. And meanwhile the parents carry on laying their trips and the now grown-up children carry on swallowing back, thinking it doesn't matter this time, and staying stuck forever. Some people change their attitudes within their first week here, some take longer – and it's not that there's a 'doctrine' here that you have to face your parents with what they've done, it simply becomes the passionate need of each person who, shifting his own body energy, needs to shake up all relationships that have become fossilized and unreal. It's no good being terribly Christian and forgiving about what's been done to you: you have to be true to yourself, that is, true to the beaten, frightened child inside who once upon a time knew for sure what he felt, knew for sure who was right and what was unjust in the world. When you tell me that instead of confronting the Christian Brother you work with who once used to beat you silly, you 'stare him in the eyes to let him know' what you feel, that is just laughable: he didn't simply stare you kids in the eyes to 'let you know' – he had more direct methods. You think you can't do anything now because everyone and everything in your environment is geared to keeping it all cool (and they don't mind how much violence they use to 'keep it cool'). It's true: if you did stand out and speak up and support the kids against the staff, there'd be a revolution, a complete upheaval. If everyone let go of their held-in energy, there'd be a complete overturning of things as we know them. But if you had a group of friends who knew you really well and cared for you and supported you, then you could do something. And that's what we give one another at Atlantis. Then you can do not just something, but anything.

The only way any of us can really be defeated is by being defeated inside. If we go the whole way in each situation, we may well all be killed eventually, but we'll die roaring – not with pain, but in defiance. Meantime, we'll be living to the full, to a full that the greys and tolerants and forgive-thems will never live. You say you have left the church, but you are still turning the other cheek. And that, unfortunately, involves turning your face away from seeing and feeling the suffering of the kids growing up now and still being bashed around by the bastards who hurt you. If just one person moved in that school, the lines would be drawn up: it's either betray the child in you and all the little people who are children now, or risk all hell let loose. Hell is hot and burns and is frightening, but it's much livelier than a meek harp-strumming heaven full of lifeless cool sanctimonious angels.

I too was an infant-teacher. One day, the head walked in and pushed and bashed the children around in front of me, pouring out the usual string of humiliations and jokes. I was incensed and nearly in tears. I followed him out of the classroom and cried in front of him and told him I never wanted him to do that again. He was kindly and patronizing and made sure he didn't do it in front of me any more. Now if I had that time again, I'd create such a racket, I'd have *him* humiliated in front of those kids. I'd lose my job, but I'd give those kids something so precious they'd never forget it – the memory of just one adult who was willing to stand up and be counted on their side.

Oh dear, I feel as if I've climbed into a pulpit. Come and have dinner with us and see the animals; they tell so much more.

Goodnight, Jenny.''

1st November, 1976
From Atlanteans in Sweden
"Dear Folks Back Home,

When we came to Sweden after six days' travelling, cold and tired and becrabbed, our last lift was not only going to Stockholm, but also to the place where Inga's father lives. This was so obviously ordained, that we went straight there, walking five exhausted and paranoid miles through the forest to get to him, and arrived late on his wedding day, which was a surprise, and found him polite and charming and more or less friendly, which was a relief, and we went to bed. The next day got heavier by degrees before breakfast, Inga growing less and less Sun-in-Taurus and more and more Aries-rising by the second, and with him sinking more and more resolutely into his embittered and stuck Scorpionic self, until the tension, after a couple of battles, several sallies and a skirmish, got so unbearable that Inga threw the wedding cake in his face, which was a joy to see. And, having missed, the plate too. And he threw us out at chair-point.

We came into Stockholm and went brawling through the streets to the Primal Cafe, which lies roughly at the centre of the 'therapy' scene here and which is almost entirely depressing with endless droning talk and theory and shared terminal misery in the atmosphere of a Calvinist service. The game is Waiting for the Therapist to come. We spoke about Atlantis and were met with uniformly scared eyes and faces – relating in the present and energetic coming-out were unknown in Sweden until our arrival and our ways are still widely suspected as interruptions of Primals-in-boxes.

Inga and I came to live here in a commune where we are six and we got into this enormous brawl which went on for hours and hours, stuck in this: 'This is a Primal Therapy Commune and we are here to clean out our feelings which means that sadly we must be relatively undefended and are therefore sorry to have to say that whilst we do hate you quite a lot it is too dangerous for our undefended selves to say more than that and we hope that eventually you'll just go away. There is the danger of psychosis.'

Eventually, we did go away, feeling like the nasties personified, embittered and totally defeated and having been threatened with physical violence by one fellow who has three months of therapy and eight years of karate to back him up.

But it was he who left the next day, and not us. What happened was this: so many people had got to dislike us by this night that there was no place left to sleep and we had to beg a bed from a passing drunk. The next day, though, Inga's friend Lena contacted us to say that she had been giving thought to all this 'coming out' and that it didn't seem a bad idea after all, and that in fact she had used it already to sort out several months' worth of heavy bad feelings about the karate expert and that he had left. Wouldn't we come and see her? We did, and have stayed since. Not that coming out with yourself has more than a limited popularity still: since the three of us came together, one person has left to be some place where he can 'primal' in peace and love, another out of fear of 'psychosis', another because he doesn't want 'heaviness' and another who was thrown out. It was quite heavy for a while – one girl came to visit and said quietly that she would like to strangle Inga and obviously meant it literally, and we pushed her to show herself more and she turned the kitchen table over and went bonkers and left.

Somewhere in the midst of all this, we decided to stay in Sweden. Despite all the heaviness and despite feeling enormously isolated and threatened, these were all 'up' days. A woman who had been to Janov came looking for Inga because she was interested in Atlantis. After two-and-a-half years with Janov and six months with a box, she was ready to pour forth enthusiasm for a commune.

Things move up and down. It's days now since I was writing to you. I've been back in the pit of despond, moaning. In fact, the house has been mostly in the pit, moaning, with no-one left to drag us out. The days I wrote about were mostly intoxicated

ones entirely filled with good feelings and enthusiasm and endless possibilities – and the up reached its top with an amazing
beautiful group with feelings pouring out and everyone really
opened. Which was a bit much to take and we all closed up
again afterwards and more or less ran off to our various holes:
Inga and I to the north to see her mother who killed us instantly
with her deathly rich food, ever-present, always-smiling insidious
niceness – killed us so thoroughly that we stayed dead quite a
while. Everything goes up and then it goes down again and then
it hovers and we come and go like a roller coaster. The intoxi-
cation came back when Hedda, the woman who was with Janov,
decided to come and live with us, bringing lots of sunshine, and
lengthening the odds against the dead silently-hating people.
We live in a permanent whirl of moved therapy rooms and half-
painted bedrooms and apple jam and sessions and people wanting to come here, though with six, the house is already really full.

In the meantime, the generosity of the Swedish state knows
no limits: you just open your mouth and make a noise and the
government asks you how much you'd like to shut it again.

I had never, ever thought to leave Atlantis, not once. It seemed
inconceivable to leave you all. But then I remember what you
said, Jenny, the day I arrived, which was that after six or seven
months, something organic happens to people and they go away,
for a while at least. And it does feel really right to be here, and
exciting and scary as well, more exposed and more sheltered
too. I feel scared as I write, as if I've gone away from my family
for the first time and need you all and don't quite know what to
say – except love to you all.

Nick."

"Dear Nick,

The primal box theory of cure is familiar to me. I was battling
against such attitudes in London years ago. One girl who had
been with me and went later to a woman trained by Janov, told
me, 'My therapist works without projection.' 'Oh does she,' I

said, 'if you were alone in a room, you'd project on to the door-knob.' There's no such thing as not projecting, of course: it just means they weren't working through their feelings for one another, nor even admitting their existence, and so were staying stuck.

In a fierce scene between my bloke Steve and this same thera-pist, she refused to engage in a real down-to-earth row and left pretending to be cool, saying, 'Look, babe, this is just my shit and your shit, OK?' In other words, let's keep clean and clear of real contact at all costs. The theory is: 'I have these strong feelings; if I get rid of them in private where no-one will react to me, I can get cured of FEELING itself, I'll never get het up about anything again and no-one will bother me.' I've said it before: primal therapy can be used as an anti-life theory. Fritz Perls had the same attitude with his, 'I am I and you are you, and if by chance we meet, that's beautiful' . . . he missed out the second half, 'and if by chance we can't stand each other's guts, we'll smile politely, won't mention it and part company speedily.' On to the next person. After all, there are millions of human beings, aren't there? And we can spend our lives skimming over all of them.

ANGER is the stumbling block. It's what everyone is scared of. Because Anger is Power and Anger is Magic. Magic is the art of changing things into something else. Anger can do that. Anger brings knees that collapse and skin that wobbles and passions that are no longer controllable. And ecstasy follows. Everyone is afraid of anger, especially the Swedes who've gone white and suicidal with it. And even Old Man Freud knew that suicide was inturned aggression. You, Nick, when you go black and arrogant, it's anger you're swallowing; and me when I go pale and silent, that's what I'm keeping down; and Pepe when he gets gooey and cajoling with Becky and we yell at him because we can all see he really wants to kill her; and Oisin when he gallops off on his black cloud.

So good luck to you both, you'll need it, to be fighting such a battle to bring red blood to such a white country. I wouldn't like to be waging that battle again. I'm glad I've converted a whole new tribe to passion-in-the-present! It's taken me years even to see the problem. I feel really glad about you daring to stir things up, and I'd love to hear more. Everyone here is really excited by your letter; I'll leave the others to tell you all the news.

With best wishes, Jenny."

Letter from Patsy
"Dear Jenny,

Maurice and I are in a horrible boat lounge with telly, one-armed bandits, booze and fags. This is what happened in Dublin:

I knew some people who were just starting a co-counselling group. We needed a place to let go of everything we were feeling and so a friend drove us to his house, gave us cushions and mattress and warned the neighbours of the noise. I spent my session realizing I'd gone dead. Maurice had to beat me (verbally!) into my feelings and we had quite a few rows before I got them back! He spent his session cursing the next door neighbour for suppressing him and also Dublin and its dead inhabitants.

After four hours, we decided to act. We went to my house; my mum was there alone with my sister's baby. She was completely dismissive, so I hit her around the face and head, beat cushions, screamed and roared for a knife saying I wanted to kill her, and she sat through it completely unmoved, throwing out smart comments saying she was sick and tired and I was waking the baby. Maurice had to push me as I felt completely taken aback at her lack of reaction after I'd hit her. My father arrived, very suppressedly aggressive, talked quietly, then lashed out viciously at Maurice, who gave him what for, while I jumped up and down and warned my mum off. Maurice ended up sitting on him. A lot of screaming and jumping went on, on my part. My father told me that understanding is more important than love and why would he be bothered with feelings? He is 'amazed at my behaviour as I was such a quiet good child and didn't need as much beating as the others.' He also said he had loved me but wouldn't be bothered saying it.

We stayed for about two hours. I just kept on and on hoping for some reaction. I was shouting and crying. When I had said all I wanted and had tried in every way to get some response, to affect them in some way, or to provoke the violence in my mother that she had always shown when I was little, I finally went for a big ashtray and threw it through the telly. They just said in an aggrieved tone: 'It's Charlie's telly.' We left. My mother walked down the drive after us with her hands out looking like a frightening ghost, saying, 'Kiss me, Patsy, kiss me.' I screamed loudly about how I hated her for all the beatings she'd given me and would never love her. It echoed nicely and I should think a good few people heard.

We ran all the way down the hill, me screaming my head off with relief and joy at smashing the telly, as they watch it every night.

All the way through, they kept saying they would have me back when I came to my senses – that I was being manipulated by Maurice like a puppet, that I was an actress, that I didn't really hate them, etc. etc. I just got angrier and angrier. At one point, my father said, 'You're just an animal!' and I said, 'Yes, I am, I'm a beautiful animal.'

On the way back to Dublin, we were kissing on the 'bus and the woman next to us was tutting and fidgeting. We asked her what was wrong and she said she'd hate to see any of her ten children behaving as disgustingly as us. I said I thought it was disgusting that she had ten kids. Then ensued a very loud and enjoyable argument about public behaviour and the rights of 'bus passengers.

Every time I think of slapping my mum and smashing the telly, I get a warm glow in my belly and I laugh. And Maurice looked delicious sitting on top of my father.

love, Patsy."

"From Maurice

The lump on me head has almost disappeared and the tingling sensation that Patsy's dad gave me in hands and feet is long gone. The blinking lights of the fair shitty are slowly receding, but I'll probably remember my first meeting with Patsy's mummy and daddy for a long long time.

The journey down here was just that – a journey down, a gradual draining of energy; a sickening coach ride of smoke and brash music echoing in our ears. We were both feeling sick; some idiot in front of us was constructing a conversation around the question, 'Do most people have the weekend off?' A woman, seen through the window, gave her teenage daughter a slap – hate, fear and a smile. A depressing conversation with Sue in Dublin about her unresolved feelings and the quietness of it all.

Fellow loonies beware! If you wander out into the dark woods of modern uncivilization, be on your guard. You can expect to have more than your sensibilities crushed! But it might not be the boot-like effect of suppressing that overwhelming desire to do obscene things with the nun's crucifix that kills you off. It may well be the million irritations, the stifling atmosphere and the silence of them all. I found myself wishing I'd never left the warmth and safety of Atlantis. I just hope this trip won't take long because I want to come home. I'm feeling a bit tearful but restrained sitting in this motorway café; the people here would be so shocked to see me crying in this plastic palace.

I feel nervous every time I think about facing my parents. I've left the place I want to make my home to visit a place that should have been. I really don't know what'll come out of it, but I'm certainly not going to get stamped on.

love, Maurice."

★ ★ ★

Late 1976 was the time of the Great Pitfall of Atlanteans, when so many communards had come face-to-face with their most terrifying depths that they preferred to 'fall down a pit' as we came to call it, rather than express all the hatred and violence in them and feel the power this gave them – and the aloneness of being powerful. We learnt so clearly how people are terrified of their own power – their power to change, to affect, to win: it is easier to go limp, go dumb and stupid, to rely on others for leadership or cues. The men seemed much more scared of their power than the women – probably because they are bigger!

I had to produce a great upsurge in myself, or be sucked under, so I appointed myself Court Jesteress. This Pit Song is the result of one of my efforts to stay alive in the creeping blackness.

THERE'S ROOM IN THE PIT FOR MORE

by JJ on her deathbed, echoed by Jill
Tune to be composed by anyone left over

Oh! Cast down your tools
and give up your chores
Give up the ghost
and get down on all fours
Crawl back to the dark
Snuff out your last spark
For there's Room in the Pit for more!
Yes! There's Room in the Pit for more!

Now Oisin was the first man
to show you all the way;
Now you can run,
There's no need to stay;
Don't face what you feel,
For comfort's more real
and anyway . . .
There's room in the pit for more,
Yes! There's room in the pit for a score.

Our Peter came after
but choked on his laughter
Tumbled head over heels
to ignore what he feels
Somersaulted twice round the therapy room
Pulled down the blinds
and spread a grey gloom.
But! No need for us all to be sore,
For – there's room in the pit for more!

Along comes sweet Clare
and lays herself bare.
'I love you, I *love* you, I LOVE YOU!' she cries.
But her poor Tony in pain
pleads, 'Don't say it again,
for your love and your caring are lies.'
Now Clare looks so pretty,
but inside she's shitty
and us lot we stand back appalled;
with Tony still waiting
and Clare still hating
for her stomach seized up and she stalled.
But! No need to abhor
Those dark days in store
For – there's room in the pit for more,
Yes! There's room in the pit for more.

It seemed at first that Johnny Joyce
(whose head was clear,
who showed no fear
who shifted readily into toppermost gear)
would lose nothing but his voice.
But alas, alack,
he turned his back
retraced his track
and lost his knack;
stayed pale and meek

and white of cheek
phased right out
without a shout
and laid back upon the floor.
But it's only fair – move over there,
And make room in the pit for more.

Now Brendie he was shining bright
Facing himself with all his might
Courageous, outrageous, he barked and he bit
Then puked it all up and fell down the Pit.
So what if I'm changing my stance?
I'd jump down the Pit at first chance.

An ill-named man is Jaimie Black,
For he's white with the strain of holding back.
No fear of him falling down the Pit –
For twenty long years he's lived in it.

Alan, teetering on the brink,
Hesitates for one more think:
'Shall I be nice and melt the ice?'
Or shall I sit here and consider it twice?
No matter if I've done it before,
There's always room in the Pit for more,
Yes, room in the Pit I ignore.

Our Patsy, she came tripping home,
Tripped and fell and turned to stone;
Hating, glaring cold as ice,
Desperately clinging to sugar and spice.
She twisted and turned to avoid a fight
But her feelings hissed out in venom and spite;
So Maurice he laid down the law
Saying: 'There's room in the Pit for more, you know,
Oh yes! There's room there so off you go!'

But Maurice himself was not quite clean,
For never fed and never weaned,
He clings and hangs and moans all day,
Refusing to cry when sent away.
Tightens his muscles and clamps his jaw,
Muttering sourly, 'I'll not thaw.'
And anyway, there's room in the Pit for More-ice,
Yes! There's room in the Pit where it's nice.

Shifting Bob
is such a job
his history I'll ignore.
Simply press the right knob,
and he'll join the pit-mob,
For there's room in the Pit for more,
Yes! There's room for blobs galore.

But Superbabe Bill is a different case:
To keep up with him, you have to run a great race;
For he tears round the room at a terrible pace.
So keep quite still, for he loves the chase.
He thrives on noise, it's one of his toys,
So just stare him calmly in the face.
He'll call you a whore
(He's a terrible bore,
Telling you things you've heard before)
Making sure never to reach his core
By covering his feelings with thoughts from his store
Of pictures of knives all covered in gore.
So just stand up to him firmly and show him the door
And tell him: There's room in the Pit for more!
Oh yes! There's room there for big babies galore.

Now our Pepe thought he was a Superdad,
The finest dad any kid ever had,
Beaming and sparkling all over the place
Keeping the blackness out of his face.

He bore up well and stuck to his role
Till faced by Beck, when he fell down a hole.
So, abandoning the mask he wore,
He made room in the Pit for more.
Yes! Sitio en un mundo sin color.

Invisible, untouchable, Hakan the Wise
Floats round the house with the moon in his eyes,
Staring, despairing, he stands at the door,
Imploring, but ignoring all that he saw.
Not learning, but yearning for days gone before.
'Oh how can I hate the mother that bore me,'
I just want you to weep as I droop and say, 'Poor me'.
Dear Hakan I'm sorry, but the result of such shit,
Is a proud place of honour, right down in the Pit.
For – there's room in the Pit for Swedes,
Yes! There's room in the Pit for weeds.

Tony from Cork is a lady's man
So strong and resilient any lady can
Just by looking at him make him so sore
That all he can gasp is, 'Room for one more?'
It's OK Tony, there's room in the pit for you,
Yes, there's room in the Pit for you too.

A really fine therapist is 'Arthur' Roy –
As long as you pretend he's just a boy.
But as soon as a woman says, 'Wow, he's a Man!'
He packed up his bags and off he ran
Yelling, 'Make room in the Pit for me!
I'm in a terrible fix, can't you see!'

We have living here a wee cannon-ball
Goes by the name of Christine Hall
Fierce as a lion though five foot tall,
Come up against her and down you'll fall.
Take care not to stroke her the wrong way or right
However you do it, she'll tense up and fight.

All you can do, though you'll end up quite raw
Is drop her firmly in the Pit –
There's room for more.

Our latest arrival is David Hughes,
A warm-hearted young man, but so confused
That when you ask him what he feels,
He curls right up and turns bum over heels.
He stands on his head,
Asks you to bed
And claims with great passion
'I FEEL DEAD!'
Punchdrunk with pain
He yells once again
'It's all YOUR shit!'
And falls down the Pit.

A special place is reserved for Joan:
Her therapy's been just one long groan.
She trundled up here hoping to scream;
Thought she could do it without being seen.
And now that it's time for our Joan to go home,
She lets out one helluver bloodcurdling Moan.
We all yawn saying, 'Babe, don't be a bore
You're so used to the Pit, you won't even feel sore.'

So me and Jill
We've had our fill
Of digging all these pits.
We're on the run
To find some fun
Instead of throwing fits.
But London Town
Will get us down,
Of that you can be sure.
So – move over please,
Two cups of teas

And room in the Pit for two more
Yes! Room to make up the full score.

So one by one
As we leave the sun
And turn to that dank dismal shore
As together we cling,
Let us sink down and sing
'There's Room in the Pit for us all,
Yes! There's room for us all to fall!'

1st December, 1976
ATLANTIS IS ALIVE AND HARRASSED AND JUST
ABOUT SURVIVING OVERRUN WITH REPORTERS AND
TV CAMERAS IN BURTONPORT, CO. DONEGAL.

3rd December, 1976
"To Elaine:
   It's happened, one of your dreams has come true. I am a
total convert to women! I didn't 'work on it', I didn't 'get into
it', I didn't sort it out or feel it out or work it out with a
speculum. The facts were just staring me in the face, and there
wasn't even a question of deciding or hesitating or pondering.
When I am dying and it is a woman who holds me; when
Atlantis is collapsing round my ear-holes and it is a woman who
builds it up; when everyone else has gone daft and it is the
women who are clear and strong and caring; then I am forced
to say: 'OK.' In spite of the fact that I never wanted to believe
my mother when she taught me that men are babies all their
lives and girls have to be grown-up from the start; in spite of
the fact that it was she who taught me: 'There may be many
men in your life, but in the end, every woman needs a woman,';
in spite of how much I have wanted to think differently from
her, I now have to say: 'There may be another world out there,
a world of truck-drivers and factory-workers and building-site
navvies and market-stall attendants, a world where the men

stand tall and strong, but in the rarified atmosphere of Atlantis, none such are to be found. Here, the women are the nurses, the mothers, the sisters, the organizers, the brains, the energy, the strength and the essence of the place. I would have died without them.' "

5th December, 1976
"Dear Babs,

I think Gaby may have got across to you on the 'phone today how the times they are a-changing.

I don't think I have cried so much, nor heard so many women cry so much, so deeply, so heartbrokenly, with so much abandon in such a short space of time in all my life. I have never held so many hurting and beautiful women in my arms. Lying in Becky's sunny room this morning, with Dory Previn singing, lying by the fire holding Chris and Patsy and all three of us sobbing, Becky doing her homework and little Marc by the window, a still-soft little man, I whispered to Patsy, 'Please write to my sister and tell her what is happening and to come here.'

That morning, I had made use of my stomach scars at last to heal: Chris thought she could never show herself, she is so damaged from carrying her son Ben; so I undressed in our women's group to encourage her, and she admitted my scars were worse! Then one by one, all the women undressed and talked about their worries about their bodies, and we looked at one another and said what we saw and what we felt. All the women are very beautiful.

The men are leaving like an epidemic. We joked that the men ought to have men's groups, but that the women would have to organize them. And that's precisely what happened: we organized the men to organize themselves. We don't need planned groups at all ourselves any more, since yesterday's group to end all groups. There has never been anything like it at Atlantis, I think the whole village must have heard. It ended at seven o'clock this morning, and is still really going on. I screamed blue murder at the total utter deadness of the sucking, pampered, limp load of male babies we have in this house sitting around waiting to be told how to live. So I told them how to live; and they sat round silent, no reaction. I was sobbing and tearing my hair out. No reaction. Silent, white faces. Wanting to murder but not willing to show it. I told them they were all scared to slap their mothers down, that they were still tied up in her skirts. Finally one or two bleeped. 'Stop nagging' nagged Cathal. The women yelled and screamed. Finally, he did try and get something together, but was immediately let down and betrayed by the other men; there is no solidarity at all amongst them.

Seven men left today! There is total revolution in the house and it is constant. There is no half-way living allowed here any more: people have to choose, and leave if they don't want to live to the full every moment. Atlantis will never be the same again. The turnover will be rapid: deados OUT. No way are we going to spend a single hour dying. We'll have Men, Women and Children here: no other categories accepted! This is going to be a focal point of energy and revolution, a spearhead of demonstrated life-force; not a long-winded sorting-out of individual karmas, but a rapid reversal of the world's deterioration. There are no gradual steps to enlightenment! You're either in it, or you're not. Atlantis is not a game or a rest-home. It's deadly serious and cosmically funny. As the numbers in the house get smaller, the energy gets higher, the lights seem brighter. We do more crying than ever before. And more laughing. The groups invariably turn into magnificent theatre. Today, we had Brendan facing Pepe with a water pistol, saying, 'Out with your feelings, or I shoot.' Yesterday, Graham turned the lights off, switched on a torch, Gaby read the narrative, Jill was Baggins and Graham was Gollum and they read the whole Gollum passage from the Hobbit, with sound effects. Idea mine, direction and execution by Graham and Gaby. Object: to get at Oisin who, after a spell of hiding in Dublin, is back physically if not emotionally. He professed not to relate to Gollum at all; his blocking didn't spoil the fun.

I have never seen so much physical violence in the house before. Fights galore, every day, real live fights. And more love than ever before. And we have exorcisms in this house. Oisin's exorcism of his father lasted three hours. It was the most powerful thing any of us had ever witnessed: madness electrified to shock and paralyse everyone who saw it. But afterwards, after you have shown and enacted what is inside you, you still have to choose. Cure is not automatic, our bodies are not machines. You can choose to live in your madness in hatred of all living creatures, or you can take your power and own up to it and use it to live and create and take command. Oisin chose the dark path, and remains haunted and stuck forever.

It's one in the morning and I can't write any more. I have cried so much. Cathal is playing my piano, Gaby is looking at my photos, Dave is cutting up cloth for cushion-fillings, and Oisin is looking unconcerned that he has lost me.

Till another day, love, Jen."

★   ★   ★

In the summer months of 1976, we had been joined by a Northern Irish couple and their two little children. They had been in contact with us for some time: they had visited the commune, read my book and our leaflets and my daughter Becky had been on holiday with them. They were very politically minded and excited by what we were doing at Atlantis, though nervous of sampling it for themselves. They recognized that like every man, woman and child on this unnaturally-organized planet, they needed help with their problems and tensions and interpersonal hassles, but were honest about how frightened they were of joining us and facing themselves. I remember clearly the day they sat in my room talking to me, deciding to bring their caravan, park it outside in the garden, and enter into Atlantean life.

I looked at them, the way they were with another, and with their children (very 'normal' – the 'normal' tenseness of every family), and I sighed mentally at what lay ahead.

'You do realize, don't you,' I warned gently, 'how explosive it's going to be coming here together, bringing the whole family unit. It's difficult enough when a person just brings himself.'

It was a big step they were taking, and I admired them for it, whilst for selfish reasons wishing they'd decided against it: I hardly relished the task ahead, knowing that when the shit starts flying, it usually flies in our direction. Still, I thought they were brave, and their plan went ahead.

It turned out it was us who had to be brave.

The wife exploded almost as soon as she moved in. It seemed we were just the excuse she had been waiting for to let go of everything. And let go she certainly did; all over us, the house, her husband and the kids. Our main task became one of containment and the establishment of boundaries, trying to introduce her to the concept of freaking out constructively instead of hysterically and unconnectedly.

It was I who gave her husband his first therapy session. As with everyone, I simply started by teaching him to breathe: that may sound strange, but we all hang on to our breathing when we're tense; we control the impact of our feelings by keeping our breathing at a minimum. If you want to loosen up, you have to learn to take air deep down into your body and let yourself melt with and flow with whatever sensation it gives you. The husband was the exact opposite of his wife; he was tight and controlled, but nonetheless full of a lifetime of held feelings swirling around confusedly inside. I remember him saying to me in his first session: 'Would I feel these things if you weren't in the room?' I smiled. He was so unused to letting energy run through his body that he actually thought I was 'doing' something to him, and that his sensations were dependent on me being there.

At that stage, he was still benevolent.

I don't know exactly when he changed, but it was very early on. Maybe he was dismayed at his wife's madness which she was letting loose all over the place; probably he didn't like the way she was standing up and getting so stroppy. All we know is, that quite suddenly, he felt it imperative, for very vague reasons, to return to Armagh, whence they came. She said NO, and the trouble started.

At first, it was quite ordinary trouble: comings and goings and persuadings and rowings; defiance and threats. Then what should have remained personal trouble was escalated out of all proportion. The husband's name was Dara Vallely, and it is to him and his friend Gery Lawless of the *Sunday World* newspaper that we owe the nickname which has stuck with us to this day: THE SCREAMERS.

Not being able to get his way with his wife, Dara simply went mad. But his way of going mad was not to shout and scream and tear his hair and cry and stamp and rage, which does nobody any harm. His way was to start inventing. And to this day, I don't know whether he believed his own inventions, or whether they were entirely malicious. I suspect the latter, as he was a well-read man.

His inventions were colourful, and at first, so we thought, harmless and ineffectual because of their obviously insane nature. We were 'a bunch of Brit infiltrators using torture techniques to brainwash people'; we 'spiked all our food with acid to produce the effects that came out of people in therapy sessions'; and 'we had taken over his wife's mind against her will.'

But when we were threatened with IRA visits, kneecappings, and were given count-downs on the telephone, with the prospect of our house being blown up, it was no longer funny. And when IRA friends and relatives of his came round, tried to snatch the baby away, broke our windows, terrorized the people in the house, and pretended to have guns, things got very alarming indeed. I was in the London commune at the time and flew home immediately, though I hate 'planes. And when the local police sat talking and smoking with Dara and his friends in cars outside our house while we were threatened in this way, we realized there was Something About Ireland that we hadn't quite reckoned with. But then, there was also Something About JJ and The Screamers that Ireland, Dara, the IRA, and the police force hadn't reckoned with. We weren't to be intimidated.

Internally, how we dealt with it was whenever any one of our number wanted to give in to fear, crumple and capitulate, they were sent upstairs immediately with a friend and told to get into their feelings mighty quick and express them privately and not spread panic around the place. One or two of the men spent most of the time of these events upstairs! Likewise, when any of our number got absurdly or indulgently aggressive, they were encouraged to get it out elsewhere, as this was hardly a time for Cowboys and Indians. Vibes not bombs win wars. And we won ours.

'SUNDAY WORLD', October 24th, 1976
MY KIDS AND THE SCREAMERS by Gery Lawless

Schoolteacher Dara Vallely spoke yesterday of his fight to save his two children from the influence of a sinister cult known popularly as 'The Screamers'.

His wife, Marietta, and children MacDara, three, and Aoife, five months, vanished last week after the High Court in London granted custody of the children to Mr. Vallely.

He said he thought the children were being hidden by members of the cult – which has its headquarters in Burtonport, Co. Donegal – in one of their English communes . . .

The cult, followers of a Californian guru figure called Arthur Janov, is known officially as 'Primal Therapy' . . .

The Vallelys, both teachers, first heard of Primal Therapy when on holiday in England. They were interested and on returning to Ireland, they exchanged letters with the Burtonport commune, visited it at Easter and arranged to return in the summer.

'Some of their ideas were interesting,' Mr. Vallely says now. 'It wasn't until you really got into it that you knew what was involved.'

The Burtonport headquarters is at Atlantis House, a rambling three-storey building, garishly painted in psychedelic designs. The cult describes it as a 'haven of sanity.'

The Vallelys went and stayed in Atlantis House in late July. 'After my first session, I felt like the top of my head was a furnace,' says Mr. Vallely. He admits that most of the cult members themselves must be sincere, but says he decided fairly quickly after experiencing it firsthand that their 'therapy' wasn't what he wanted for his family. Marietta, however, had become a fervent convert and adamantly refused to leave.

Gery Lawless spoke to her at the Villa Road Commune in Brixton before she disappeared . . . She said that after the disagreement in August about whether to stay on in Atlantis House, the cult had arranged a 'confrontation' where she, her husband, and members of the commune discussed the problem. 'We attempted to get Dara to say what was really on his mind, but failed,' she said.

Mr. Vallely returned the next day, she said, with members of his family and her own family and tried to take the children. During the attempt, a window of Atlantis House was broken. The following day, her husband came back again, this time with Gardai, and once more tried to persuade her to come back to Armagh with him and bring the children. It was after this that she flew to the cult's London base at Villa Road.

She arrived in London 'a totally different person', according to a member of her family who met her. 'She was totally hostile to the people she had been closest to, and seemed to trust no-one but people from Primal Therapy. She had a completely different personality. It was as if she had been brainwashed by this thing.'

1st November, 1976

"Dear Marietta,

The forces of the Outside are closing in all right, but if you feel guilty about the *Sunday World* article, don't worry. You can't do something genuinely revolutionary without getting comeback. The forces for and against life are being polarized.

In the night, I am scared sometimes, but in the daytime, I am in fighting spirit, and that means enjoying myself. I am slowly

recovering from two days spent away from here. Sickness was
all around: 'radicals' still going to Mass and living with Mummy
and no-one fighting, everyone keeping safe. But we have been
asked to return to speak at the university and to write articles,
and we certainly stirred up some interest. The world has already
been ruined, so all we can do is put all our energy into preserv-
ing what life there is in and around us. The other side will
undoubtedly win in the end, because they're willing to use guns;
but we'll enjoy dying with a big scream that will have echoes!

love, Jenny."

6th November, 1976
"Dear Marietta,

Your experiences at the psychotherapy workshop in Scotland
ring loud bells for me. I just love to hear about you standing up
for lively therapy in all innocence expecting a good reception!
I once did a huge group there during the 'psychology' week, and
in the end, the 'left-wing' organizers sent a load of heavies in to
try and stop us, because real things were happening between
people instead of the usual sitting around talking about the far-
distant possibility of things happening. I'd love to have seen their
faces with you sparking and buzzing all over the place.

Here we are becoming more and more politically involved,
quite without seeking it. Myself, Oisin and Maurice regularly
produce horrific nightmares about what there is in store for us.
During the dark hours, I shudder and shake and think, 'I'll give
it up, I'll tone it down, I'll play safe'; that's how scared I am.
But by the time the morning light comes, all the ghosties and
ghoulies and long-leggity beasties have flown from my brain,
leaving a few cobwebs and bruises, but I'm up again fighting
and enjoying what we're doing.

Another nightfull is awaiting me now, and so is Oisin, so I'll
say goodbye."

★   ★   ★

'DAILY MIRROR', November 17th, 1976
CULT OF THE SCREAMERS
" 'Probe This Strange Sect', pleads Deputy

An inquiry is to be urged today into the strange cult known as the Screamers. The appeal will be made to the Dail (Irish Parliament) by the Deputy Opposition Leader, Joe Brennan. He will question two Cabinet Ministers about the activities of the sect . . . (which is) in the heart of Mr. Brennan's constituency . . . 'There is great anxiety and concern among local people about what is going on and about the activities of these people.'

He added, 'Certain considerations are involved. One of these is about people setting up a house for psychiatric treatment. Who are they? Have they got a license?

'I want the whole matter investigated and brought out into the open. This should be done as quickly as possible because of the local concern.'

Mr. Brennan's Parliamentary questions are to Justice Minister Patrick Cooney and Health Minister and Deputy Premier Brendan Corish.

He is asking Mr. Cooney if he is aware of the group in Burtonport, whether they are Irish citizens or aliens, and if the police have carried out investigations to determine whether they are involved in any illicit activities . . .'

We Have Nothing To Hide
The leader of the Screamers, 34-year-old Kent-born Jenny James last night issued an invitation to Mr. Brennan.

'Come and see what is going on,' she said.

'This house is completely open to anyone. I would welcome Mr. Brennan if he decided to come in and have a look for himself.'

She said she was not worried about the Dail questions."

★   ★   ★

" 'DEPORT THE SCREAMERS', Says Doctor

A strange cult known as the Screamers should be deported from the Republic, a doctor-politician said last night.

'They strike me as a bizarre group who are only attracting drop-outs,' said Dr. Hugh Byrne, Fine Gael, TD (MP) in Dublin.

Dr. Byrne said, 'I am alarmed that they are allowed to carry on with their so-called primal therapy.'

'Speaking as a doctor, I have to insist that this is not a qualified type of treatment.'

Two Cabinet Ministers defended the cult when questions were raised in the Dail last week.

Health Minister and Deputy Premier Brendan Corish said the group's activities did not seem to come under the scope of the Mental Treatment Act.

And Justice Minister Patrick Cooney said he was not aware that the law was being broken.

Dr. Byrne said, 'I am not satisfied with these answers and intend raising the matter again in the Dail.'

'I see no reason why these people cannot be investigated by the police and health authorities.' "

★ ★ ★

'SUNDAY WORLD', 21st November, 1976
SCREAMERS ROW: NOW MERLYN REES WILL BE QUIZZED

"The Donegal-based cult known as 'The Screamers' – which was given a clean bill of health in the Dail last Wednesday – has now become the subject of controversy at Westminster.

Next week, Armagh Unionist MP, Harold McCusker is to ask the Home Secretary Merlyn Rees a series of questions about the cult's activities and its possible involvement in the disappearance of an Armagh woman, Marietta Vallely and her two young children.

Mr. McCusker told the *Sunday World* yesterday: 'From the little I have learned about this dangerous organization, I am amazed that the authorities in the Republic have allowed it to become established and to prosper.'

The Independent MP for Fermanagh-South Tyrone, Mr. Frank Maguire, has also seen Mr. Rees to press for an enquiry."

★ ★ ★

'THE SUNDAY PRESS', November 21st, 1976
INSIDE THE HOUSE OF THE SCREAMERS
Report: Eanna Brophy
They Laugh at the Rumours
"There is a standing invitation to Fianna Fail's Deputy Leader, Joe Brennan, TD, or anyone else who is interested, to visit the mysterious-looking house called 'Atlantis' in the Donegal fishing village of Burtonport.

The term 'cult' and 'sect' and, of course, 'Screamers' have been attached to the people who live there in recent weeks, since Armagh teacher Dara Vallely blamed them and their counterparts in London for the disappearance of his wife and two children. But when I called there this week, I found nothing mysterious or terrifying about the occupants of Atlantis.

It was raining heavily when we arrived outside the big, forbidding 12-roomed house in Burtonport. The outside walls are painted with astrological symbols and other designs on a bright green background. Making our way past a yellow van and several damp but friendly dogs, we called to the side door, not quite knowing what to expect.

We were greeted by 34-year-old Jenny James from Kent, a cheerful, attractive woman who instantly welcomed us in, gave us tea, introduced us to some of the other occupants and offered to answer any questions we cared to ask.

One's first impression is that there is nothing very 'cultish' about the Atlantis people. They bear little resemblance to the various odd religious sects that have appeared and disappeared on the Irish scene in the past few years.

And so far as one could gather from a brief visit, there is little evidence that anyone is 'brainwashed' into staying there. We were told that people come and go all the time.

With one or two exceptions, they seemed an extrovert lot, eager to talk, about themselves and their life-style, and also to joke about their recently-acquired image. One cartoon stuck up on the wall was a drawing of a grim, dark building, signposted, 'Scream Inn – we're only here for the fear.'

In fact, the Primal Therapy Community, as they prefer to be called, do scream. One of them was doing quite a lot of it behind closed doors when we went on a tour of the building. Jenny James pointed out that that is only a small part of what they do. They also laugh a lot, as we saw. The man who was screaming during our visit was jokingly described as 'one of our best screamers'.

As we spoke in the kitchen, other occupants, male and female, drifted in. About half of the 25-strong commune are Irish. Most of the rest are English, though there are also Germans, Swedes and two newly-arrived French-Canadians. They all looked surprisingly conventional. About 90% of them are from Catholic backgrounds, though few of them believe in any religion now.

We spoke to one of them who has a university degree. He came to Atlantis a year ago because he found that he could not relate properly to other adults, male or female. He blamed this on his repressed life at home and at school while growing up, which he now recalls as being dominated by violence and lack of communication on the part of his teachers and parents . . .

At one point, as he talked to us, he broke down and wept openly and unashamedly, but a few minutes later he had recovered and went on talking. His parents are seeking a court injunction to stop him making accusations against them. But his description of his upbringing does not differ greatly from that of many others who have been through the Irish educational mill.

Other Irish visitors to Atlantis told stories similar to him, though not as articulately or emotionally. Tom Kelly from Carlow remembers his young life as a grey existence and feels he has found his first real friends in the Burtonport commune.

And Cathal Black, formerly an RTE cameraman, also said that he could not form real relationships with other adults until he came here. He was working on a television film of a John McGahern story when he began to realize that his own life was not very fulfilling.

Two former journalists from England, photographer Roy Wilson, and writer Peter Wanless, told us they had both led more or less conventional middle-class lives in England for several years, but felt vaguely that there was something missing until they came in contact with the Primal Therapy Movement.

Roland Turenne from Quebec and his girlfriend Francine, arrived in Atlantis only a few days ago, after visiting other communes in Europe and Britain. They didn't yet know whether they would stay on there.

Asked about the Vallely family, Jenny James says the Primal Therapy Movement accepts no responsibility for breaking up the family. 'As far as we are concerned, they came here and Mrs. Vallely decided she liked what we were doing and her husband did not. There was absolutely no pressure from us either way. Whatever Mrs. Vallely has done since then is her own decision and does not involve us.' "

★ ★ ★

'Sunday Mirror'
SCREAMERS DEFY BOMB THREAT BY IRA
by James Dunne
CULT WHO LIVE IN FEAR

"In a rambling 18-roomed former hotel in a quiet fishing village, a mysterious cult nicknamed the Screamers live out a strange daily routine. What sort of people are they? Is there a sinister background to their affairs? Today the *Sunday Mirror* presents the startling facts in a special investigation.

A strange cult nicknamed the Screamers revealed to me this week how they are living in fear.

They say the IRA have threatened to bomb their 18-roomed home, which has already had windows broken.

Members claim they have been warned of kneecapping if they don't get out. But the thirty people who live in the colourful house in the tiny fishing village of Burtonport have refused to leave.

Jenny James, who set up the commune over a year ago, said yesterday, 'We have no intention of leaving. Of course we are frightened, but we have learned to cope with fear.

'We intend to expand our commune, not close it down. We are not harming anyone. The IRA are responsible for the threats but we have talked it over and are determined to carry on.' "

★   ★   ★

19th December, 1976   Atlantis
"Dear Jenny,

On Saturday morning, Tigger-dog suddenly lept up at the bedroom window and started wagging her tail. I looked out and saw two men at the bottom of the driveway – they signalled to a third in the road who then signalled to the rest. As soon as I saw them, I thought it was Dara come with his IRA friends, but just as quickly, I knew it was a drug raid. I went to wake Clare and Brendan and was just coming out of their room when there were swarms of police all over the house – fifteen at least. We were ordered to our rooms and the search began. Clare was hustled into the bathroom with a woman officer to dress; two started searching my room but were quickly called over to Christine who was yelling and screaming at having to get dressed in front of a male and wanting a piss. The women fuzz escorted her to the loo. I feel good about her not letting them push her around.

After quite a long time, we all congregated in the 'Boys' room' and the superintendent comes in to quiz us about our 'sex orgies' and says he has photos of them! We said we knew nothing of any photos and would he like to show us them. He just laughed and said we were probably in them. I kept pushing for him to show us and right at the end, he dismissed the subject saying, 'Let's forget about it,' and walked out. Looking through your photo album afterwards, Jenny, we found some photos of you, Frank, Gino and Joan naked in the therapy room – written on the back of one was 'a typical Atlantean Orgy, Summer '75'. Quite a laugh!

They also made lots of snide remarks about the contraceptives they found, and the books on sex. Afterwards, we found the photo of Becky receiving her cycling proficiency award with two policemen in the picture left on show on your typewriter – another snide message. I also found a cigarette end stubbed out on one of your wooden cabinets. I feel totally disgusted. They had read lots of your letters and generally snooped around. They went on to the island too and the inspector asked Pepe if it was true that Becky had been raped on the island in the summer! He was astounded and said, 'No'. I got the feel from this and lots of their questioning that they were trying to pin something on us about not looking after the children 'properly'. They said to Pepe as they left that they were satisfied that there was nothing here in the way of drugs, and yet we were on the RTE news and in the newspapers with the police saying they had 'taken pills and some other substances from the house.' I guess their chemists will enjoy themselves analysing lavender, pot-pourri, raspberry leaves, aspirin and Graham's hay-fever pills! They even took some henna.

We're cleaning up the whole house – the police left everything in a right mess after the raid. That's all for now.

Love to you, Jill."

★ ★ ★

'DONEGAL DEMOCRAT', Friday, 24th December, 1976
GARDAI AND DRUG SQUAD RAID 'SCREAMERS' HOME
Pills, Powders and Herbs Removed
"In a sensational raid on Saturday morning, nineteen Gardai and drug squad detectives under Supt. John Gurhy, Glenties, swooped on the house known as Atlantis, the home of the sect which has earned the nickname 'Screamers' and carried out a thorough search for drugs. The four houses, property of the sect

on Inishfree Island off Burtonport, were also searched and a quantity of pills, powders and herb-like substances were removed for examination.

At about 10.45 a.m., the six-car strong convoy of garda cars pulled into Burtonport and parked behind trees on the main road leading past 'Atlantis'. The plain clothes detectives accompanied Supt. Gurhy as with Inspector Deasy and Sergeant Joe Farrell of Burtonport, they approached a door at the seaward side of the house, obviously the door most in use by the inhabitants.

The knock on the door was answered by the oldest resident of the house, Pepe Garcia, who is in his forties. Mr. Garcia was shown a warrant and was informed that the gardai were about to search the house on the warrant which was issued under the Dangerous Drugs Act, 1934. All the gardai then entered the house and a systematic search, which was to last for an hour-and-a-half began. Most of the inhabitants of the house were still in bed and they were woken and informed that the house was being searched.

One room was examined and as each of the residents was searched, they were sent to that room and ordered to remain there while the rest of the house was examined. Spokeswoman for the members, Gillian Tomlinson (30), formerly of Wiltshire, England, told our reporter that it was a most unpleasant experience on waking to find a detective in her room. She was not told what was going on, but she put 'two and two together.' . . . Asked if the raid would make any difference to the community, Gillian said that she did not think so. 'Our doors are open to anyone. We have had the television cameras in here and reporters and everyone,' she said . . .

At the conclusion of the searches in the house, gardai confiscated a collection of pills and plastic bags containing a herb-like substance. Members of the commune described these as medicines and multi-vitamins, raspberry leaf tea and lavender. It is understood also that the passports of a French-Canadian couple were also confiscated as it appeared that they had entered the

Republic through the Six Counties without reporting to immigration control . . .

In a statement after the raid, Supt. Gurhy said 19 gardai had been involved . . . The object of the search was to ascertain whether or not there were drugs on the premises. Samples of substances were taken solely for analysis purposes, he said, adding that gardai were satisfied that none of the residents were actively participating of drugs. No arrests were made. A total of 14 members of the commune were present during the raid.

A member of the Burtonport Residents' Committee, Mr. Cathal Murray, said that the 'Screamers' were no longer welcome in Donegal. 'People here are living in fear of them and we want them out – we want to live in peace,' he said, adding that telegrams had been sent to Government ministers demanding that the sect be asked to leave."

★ ★ ★

'DONEGAL DEMOCRAT'
Readers' Letters Page
"Sir,

Regarding the letter in the recent issue of your paper, written by Sean O'Cearnaigh, Annagry, it is gratifying to find a person to give an objective evaluation on the 'Screamers'. Here we have a minority living in a so-called Christian community being victimized for their beliefs at a time when we are being so vocal in condemnation of oppression of the Catholic minority in Northern Ireland.

Surely this is a ridiculous state of affairs when we ourselves oppress people less fortunate than ourselves. The people have been living at Burtonport for some time and there have been no complaints about them until the matter was raised in the Dail by Mr. Brennan. As far as I am aware, the Gardai had no reason to suspect them of carrying on any sinister activities. It is surprising that the Garda raid occurred shortly after this political mud-slinging. The Gardai in this case have been used as political pawns to satisfy politicians. Law enforcements should be left to the police. Politics have no place in law enforcements because to allow this would lead to corruption as has happened in other spheres.

I resent very much, as a member of the Garda Siochana (the Irish Police) that we should be used as political pawns. The Garda raid on the 'Screamers' has portrayed the gardai as oppressors. I would like to add that this is not so. The gardai were unwilling partners in this operation which was forced on them from the political arena.

Yours, 'Anonymous.' "

★　★　★

"Dear Jill,

Don't worry about all the newspaper reports. The main thing I want you all to do is laugh whenever anyone refers to the possibility of us leaving, and dismiss it out of hand, saying there's no question of it, it's our home and there's nothing anyone can do to move us. Please send me all the Irish post that comes, just out of interest, as my heart is always with the revolution in Ireland, and I want to keep in touch with the climate!

love, Jen."

★　★　★

"Dear Jenny,

We keep getting poisonous anonymous letters and Christmas cards, saying that if we believed in the Good Lord, we would be saved!

We are warm and snug inside Atlantis, though, so to hell with the Outside. I miss the women's groups and chats in your room, but the house is looking and feeling good and your spirit is here.

I want to tell you that you were one of the first people to see me and to give to me and not expect me to give first. This means the whole world to me because I feel your passion and feel it clear like an unspoiled mountain stream and know it is honest and true.

I love the environment and all animals great and small because I can see and feel them – the wind, the rain, the sun, the sea, the smell of everything, has in the past given me more than people. I can feel myself in the wind, but I so seldom feel people. Here at Atlantis, I have, but as I let more people into me, more of them abuse me and it is hard to keep opening up.

A witchy friend of mine told me something once which always stuck in my mind: something about how the witches must have laughed when they added Hope to Pandora's box, because hope is the worst evil of them all, as it is hope that drives men to endure the bitterest misery in the world right to the very end.

Daily my hope sinks as the pit grows bigger, but I feel there is another kind of hope – a sunlight and a passion that I feel from you, Jenny, always, and that I feel in myself a little; and it is growing bigger in spite of all the shit around, as I feel myself growing. The best thing I have been given in the world came to me through being Graham's girlfriend and that was to come to Atlantis and know and love you. I know I have already developed lots from being here, especially without you so close, as it has made me feel and use my own strength more. At the same time, I wouldn't be able to do without your constant supply of energetic letters that tell me so much, give me so much, and make me feel even more.

Jill."

★   ★   ★

Anonymous Christmas Card
"It makes me feel sad every time I think of you all up there. What a waste of a precious life. God loves you all and had some purpose of putting you and friends into the world. This screaming may relieve in some way, but the good Lord has better plans for us all.

Please do greet the birth of Christ in some other way. You will find if you and your friends all got together on Christmas night and visited the local church and welcome the new King, you would find more happiness than I could explain. We all celebrate Christmas. Why? Let those neighbours who are scared of you see at Christmas that you believe in Christ and we must see the person of Christ in all fellow men. I was brought up in a Catholic happy home, today my children are married in happy homes, that's why my heart bleeds for you boys and girls. If you would only turn to Christ this Christmas, I feel He would give you the blessings you need.

I will pray for you all at midnight mass at Christmas. He suffered in life for our sakes, please try to offer all your past sufferings with the sufferings of Christ and He will repay you.

This crying and screaming is really sad when you could be doing so much good otherwise and if life was unkind in the past, do try to make a better future."

★   ★   ★

IRISH PARENTS SPEAK

"My dear Mary,

I have read and re-read your letter, honey, and I am nearly sick with worry having read it, and I thank the good and merciful Lord that Mammy did not get her hands on it as it would most surely have sent her straight into hospital again. Mary darling, would you please I beg of you, please tell me that the place you are in is not some sort of nursing home or something like that. Oh god forbid that you have been ill and had some sort of nervous breakdown. What are they doing to you in that place you are in? I beg of you to please come home before I get a nervous breakdown myself and have to go into hospital too. Oh my god darling, I wish you knew how serious I am about this – do you want me to go up to see you and would you come down with me if I did go up? Please tell me if you have been ill. Oh what sort of place are you in at all? Are you all right? For god's sake honey, 'phone us or write immediately you get this letter as I am worried sick – what in god's name have they done to you up there in that awful place? Please come home for god's sake or do you want me or would you like me to go for you, anything so long as I know that you are all right and not ill.

Mary darling, Mammy does not even know that I am writing to you and it was only by the mercy of god that I got the post this morning. If she had gotten that letter of yours, it would most surely have put her back in hospital, not because of any blackmail or any other motive but because Mary honey we plain and simply love you and miss you so very much, just as we always have and always will although we may have a funny way of displaying our love at times. Mary darling, please I beg of you, don't take ten years off my life and please tell me that you are not ill. Honey how could you ever say that we ever hated you and loved your sister or any other member of the family? I am crying like a baby as I write this letter, asking myself where have I gone wrong as a father. Mary honey, your good mother and I have always and always will love you just as we love all of our family. We have never made fish of one and flesh of the other and all I can say to you is I am begging you now before you break both our hearts to please come home even for a little while and if you think you have been badly treated, then please give us a chance to make up for it even for a short while. I am nearly sick with worry that you are ill. Is the place you are in some sort of nursing home? I don't know what I am writing to you, I am so worried darling, how could you ever say that we hated you or were angry with you and so on.

Mammy and I are just plain simple people – we never had much of our own and is it a crime or a sin for us to want to give our children the very best we could give them with our limited resources? Mary darling before I go crazy with worry, will you please write or 'phone immediately and tell me that you are not ill. If Mammy even saw your letter, it would break her heart, particularly because in her own muddled stupid unselfish way she loves you and god knows honey, I do too. Where did we go wrong? If I don't hear from you in some way within the next few days that you are really all right, I will have to 'phone the garda in Burtonport or go up there myself before I go crazy with worry. When you mentioned in your letter that Atlantis is a place of primal therapy, my heart nearly stopped and I got physically sick. Oh my god honey, are you all right? I don't know how I am going to contain myself until I hear from you again. If I have done anything to hurt you, I pray and beg that you and god will forgive me. For god's sake honey, please write by return or 'phone us that you are all right and please, please, I am begging you to please come home if only for a short while. I have told you so often how I miss you. What do I have to do, honey, to prove it and to prove that I am so very fond of you? I pray to god and his holy mother nothing is wrong with you. Please reply, remember honey, I am so worried.

All my love, Dad."

Around this same time, the local police 'phoned Atlantis asking for confirmation that Mary would be "allowed out" to contact her parents if she so desired.

What had Mary written to bring on this reaction?

"Dear Mum and Dad,

I have known for some time that I have avoided telling you the truth about my life, about what I believe and where my opinions and ideas differ from yours. Why? Because I have been afraid of you, afraid of your reaction. If I came out against you when I was young, you threatened me with your anger – with Dad behind you – and now you threaten me with saying you will commit suicide or get very sick.

Well, I am tired of the pretence of our family and refuse to continue that way any more. I think it is time I came out honestly with what I feel and not sit there and allow you to state the law in the house.

When I was a child, I needed love from you both. When I did not feel loved, I started acting as a nice good little girl in order to get it. I started doing things for you, Mum, so that you would love me for it. Right now, I feel angry that I had to prove that I was worth loving.

Mum and Dad, I don't really expect you to understand this right off, but maybe you will in the future. I am sure you did not expect your children to remain dummies forever. You tried to show us and give us your way of life – you thought it was the best we could get because it was all you knew. Mum, don't get sick; Dad, don't just get angry. I am asking from you now to give me room to breathe, room to find my best kind of life and my place in the world. I have not gone crazy and this is not a 'phase' I am going through. It has taken me a long time to get the courage up to write this letter. I would like to start a more meaningful relationship with you both.

Once again, Mum, I will ask you: don't tell me you are going to get sick, as I consider you are trying to blackmail me into coming and looking after you.

Mary."

A few days later, Mary's parents turned up at Atlantis. Mary happened to be forty miles away in Letterkenny hospital, as she had cut her face badly falling off a bicycle. Her parents would not believe she wasn't here and were extremely hostile and insulting. Mary 'phoned them that night complaining about this. And she replied to her father's first letter as follows:

"Dear Father,

My reaction to your letter has been extreme anger. The letter I wrote to you was to you both and first I would like you to show that letter to my mother right now. If I do not get a reply from her, I will write again and again and unless you want to get up and get the post every morning, I suggest you show it to her. If I do not get a letter soon, I will write to one of our neighbours and ask them to pass it on.

I am not sick or in a nursing home, nor have I had what you would call a nervous breakdown. What I have done and am doing is coming out with what I feel for the first time. The place I am living in is a primal therapy commune and I came here of my own free will and I most certainly would not like you to come up and collect me, nor do I feel like going home.

You ask yourself what you did wrong as a father. Well, I will tell you. Never in all the time that I lived with you could I come to you for anything. Yes, you gave me money and clothes and things like that – but there is more to being a father than being a material provider. I never once felt as a child that I could go to you for love, warmth or even a touch from you. I was told by you and Mum, 'leave your father be, he has worked all day and now he is tired.' When I was a child, I thought fathers were men who went out to work and earned money. But I still needed love, so I went to my brother, and when he rejected me, I went to other men and have been doing so since, carrying this huge need with me and laying it on their shoulders. I have spent my life looking for the father I never had.

Your letter right now makes me sick and angry as you expect me to forget all that and to love you. Well, Dad, I don't. Don't keep pretending. I don't really believe you feel strongly for me. What you write reeks of guilt. As far as my relationship with you is concerned, I would like to straighten things out. I don't want any more letters like the one you just sent me – coming out with all this love and honey stuff. What you are really saying is that you don't want Mum to know. I have not forgotten all those years of how you sat in your chair, gruff and silent and making sure through brute force that we did not disturb you. How can you pretend that you loved me then, when you did not even ever once ask me how I felt? If you did not love me then, how can you now? I just don't believe you. If by chance you do feel guilty, you can make it up in your own way, but don't let us pretend there is any love between us. As to the continuation of our relationship, all I will say is, don't tell me what to do.

I will sort out my own relationship with Mum – and then it is up to you both to sort things out between yourselves. You are only making things worse by hiding that letter from her, because I am determined to bring things out into the open between us all.

Mary

PS If you want to know more about primal therapy, you can read a book called 'The Primal Scream' by Arthur Janov."

"Dear Mary,

I got your letter this morning which has finally put the lid on things after your 'phone-call last night, if one could call it a 'phone-call. I have tried to be patient and to understand what you are trying to tell me, but at last my patience is exhausted and for a change now I too am very angry. You proved to me last night with your abusive 'phone-call that you have absolutely no concern for your mother or her feelings – what you think about me is not of the slightest importance to me any more. You showed absolutely no concern whatever for the fact that since we got your letter on Monday, your good mother has been in an APPALLING STATE OF GENUINE DISTRESS and is now GENUINELY ON THE VERGE OF A NERVOUS BREAKDOWN. You showed no concern whatever for the fact that she has not slept one wink since Monday night or that out of sheer honest love and concern that she got out of bed yesterday morning at 5 a.m. and drove 240 miles to see you. You are only concerned with the fact that our visit has disturbed your hippy friends – then you have the colossal cheek and impertinence to talk to me about love. I do not have to be told about love by some cheap sick quack in a cheap paperback book. You don't know a single thing about love or parenthood or staying up all night nursing a sick child, going without things yourself to provide for one's children, your mother starving herself to provide pocket-money for you and buy you clothes, etc. What the hell would you know about love – cheap dirty sex perhaps with your cheap shoddy second-hand quotations about love from cheap shoddy paperback books written by sick neurotic drop-outs and I do not have to justify myself to you. How dare you. You have the cheek to talk to me about blackmail in your first letter – something about blackmailing you into loving us. What may I ask would you call your letter that came this morning with your threat to keep annoying us with your letters and annoying our neighbours? Once and for all time to come, Mammy has now read your letter and is replying to it even though it again caused her great distress and I warn you right now Mary of two things:

1. You are obviously a very sick and bitter girl and may god forgive you for that and if you write just one more letter even that upsets Mammy or bothers a neighbour, I shall take you and that whole colony to court on a charge of plain aggravation, disturbing the peace and denial of constitutional rights, and don't think I won't do it. I am now so angry with you and have lost my patience so much with you that I will do anything.

2. You are obviously god help you at the moment a terribly sick girl and if you continue to pester and annoy us or our neighbours with your letters and your so-called imaginary crack-pot grievances, I shall have you committed to a proper nursing home for psychiatric treatment which I can do as your father. I have checked this with a solicitor. For your own sake, don't drive me to that. Whether I do so or not depends on yourself. As your father, I can have you committed as you are obviously in need of proper treatment, so for your own sake stop writing these threatening blackmailing letters which I shall keep for the psychiatrist. You see, Mary, your only trouble is that you cannot and will not face life and reality and grow up. What the hell would you know about love or parenthood or caring for people when all of your rational semi-adult and adult life you have just thought of yourself, your own crazy mixed-up ideas (the latest effort Atlantis cops the lot). You are utterly incapable of decent normal human feelings towards your parents. You can preach whatever claptrap psychiatric second-hand tripe you like to me, but I warn you if there is even one more letter to this house on the same lines as your last two efforts, or if you annoy, worry or threaten your mother in any way (it runs off me like water off a duck because I know you are sick) and only looking for notice as you are a failure and can't cope with normal life, then I shall seriously consider having you committed to a hospital if you write even once more in a similar vein or annoy our neighbours.

Before you kill your good mother with worry, why don't you go and see a doctor before I get desperate and have to do it for you. Otherwise, get a grip on yourself and try and be adult and face life. I have discussed your commital to a hospital with Mammy and she agrees with me that it would be the best thing for you, so I will give you just one more chance to stop writing those foolish letters and try to be a rational normal human being and not trot out these stupid idiotic second-hand clichés adnauseam. I will not have you pestering your mother and we do not give a twopenny damn whether you are angry or not. If you continue to give us trouble, I will as I have said, have you committed as I am afraid you are definitely in need of medical attention.

As you seem to have become utterly heartless, I now say to you: how dare you upset your unfortunate mother in such a fashion. Good god, Mary, have you got any heart in you at all? If you could only see your mother since Monday last and what you have done to her. I promise you here and now Mary, that if Mammy has to go into hospital again or god forbid that worse should happen, I will make you wish that you were never born. How could you act in such a manner towards your mother? As regards me, do not put the blame for your own failures on my shoulders. You got a normal decent healthy upbringing. You got plenty of love just like any child gets, despite your denial to the contrary, and you are just trying to put the blame on my shoulders. You had every chance in life, but up to now you have gone from bad to worse trying to prove something to yourself. Mary, do you realize where you are heading and how really sick you must be? Before it is too late, get a grip on yourself and pray hard just as we are praying hard for you. It does help, you know. I don't profess to be even a good Christian and I may be even a hypocrite in your eyes and like all poor souls who can't cope, you may consider religion a lot of balderdash, but I have found personally that prayer is a great help. Even I, a dreadful sinner, have had requests answered and I try to go to Mass every day – try it sometime."

The very next day, the following arrived, headed in red ink:
AS THIS MAY BE THE MOST IMPORTANT LETTER
OF YOUR LIFE, FOR ALL OUR SAKES BUT MOST
PARTICULARLY FOR YOURSELF, PLEASE READ ALL
OF IT PATIENTLY BEFORE YOU SAY OR DO ANY-
THING. *DON'T SHUN THE TRUTH.* THE CON-
SEQUENCES ARE TOO AWFUL TO CONTEMPLATE.

"Dear Mary,
    I have very deliberately waited to give all concerned plenty
of time to think calmly before I write to you what is going to
be my last letter to you until you come to your senses and stop
blaming other people for your weaknesses and misfortunes. This
may be (and I am not being melodramatic) the most important
letter that you will ever get or ever read in your whole life and
despite the fact that it may be a little unpalatable to you in
places, I would ask you for your own sake and the sake of your
family to think very hard and very carefully before you go off
half-cocked again.
    This is going to be a straightforward, honest and sincere
letter and an awful lot is going to depend on how you take it and
I do hope that all your moral courage is not completely gone
and that you have even a tiny spark of human decency left in
you. I am not begging or whining or pleading – what you are
getting is straight facts and I am not suffering from any guilt
complex (I first heard that expression in 1939) because I have
nothing to feel guilty about except perhaps the obvious fact that
Mammy and I spoiled you rotten, nor do I harbour any anger
or resentment against you or your so-called tragic friends up in
that unfortunate hellhole. I have now gotten over the initial
shock of complete disgust and anger that any daughter of mine
could debauch and degrade herself so much and attack her
parents to cover up her own obvious guilt and complete failure
to have the decency and moral courage to fight with and cope
with the rotten world we live in and run away and hide and give
up life in an appalling place like that.

As I have already said, the only 'guilt' that Mammy or I may
feel is that we spoiled you and gave you far too much love, too
much latitude and too much consideration at the expense of the
rest of the family and it is very hard to take, particularly for
your good mother (whom you are driving to an early grave),
that anything we did for you does not appear to have been
appreciated even in the slightest degree, and no excuses or
attacks by you (to cover up your rotten and shameful act) can
ever change what is a plain honest fact and candidly, Mary,
even you must know that there is a god in heaven despite how
you may sneer and jeer to the contrary, and you know equally
well that you will never know an hour's peace or real happiness
for what you are doing, particularly to your mother. I have seen
the toughest hard cases sneer and jeer at the church and at god
and blame the church for their failures, but my god I have seen
personally one such hard nut scream and weep and beg for a
priest as he lay dying on the roadside in a bad car smash. I don't
have to go beyond your own sister who also sneered at religion
but the night before her operation in hospital, she was a very
normal and frightened girl and never stopped telling us afterwards how good she felt after the priest had been with her.

Now, Mary, you can tear up this letter if you like. You need
not answer it if you like (you probably won't because you can't
stand the truth), and if you feel so inclined, you may not talk
to us or write to us ever again, but just as your unfortunate
grief-stricken mother is, I am praying hard that there is still left
in you just even one tiny spark of human decency and com-
passion (there can't be any love in you for what you have done)
and I am therefore making this one final effort with no abuse,
vilification or rebukes – just plain simple honest facts which you
must agree with if you are at all honest. What I am going to say
to you and talk to you about does not come out of any cheap
dog-eared paperback mumbo-jumbo and psychiatric clichés and
rubbish usually written by some sick soul or head case who
retreated from the world because he or she had no guts. These
people usually wind up anyway in the nuthouse or worse, god

help us, by hanging themselves or commit suicide, making thereby a hell in the hereafter as well as on earth for themselves and all whom they unfortunately contaminate.

You see, Mary, being your father and a man who has loved and cared for you all these years (despite what your guilty conscience makes you protest to the contrary), I can read you like the proverbial book and know every little change in your mood and you are as predictable as our rotten weather and you resent this fact so much that you use me as a scapegoat for your degrading conduct and turn on me like a mad dog. Hence all this stupid rubbish and tenth-rate old hat clichés from the cheap paperback (written by some jaded junky) about being angry at me for the first time in your life etc., telling me that I am fawning on you, whinging because I have a guilt complex, trying to come between me and your mother and my wife because, sad to say and tragically, you are so unhappy yourself. I do not suffer, Mary, from any complex in the *slightest*. As I have said, Mary, you are so predictable it amazes me and I am truly and sincerely sorry for you that up to now you have made a bit of a mess of your life but that should not stop you from having the moral courage now before it is tragically too late, to pick up the few pieces that are left, kick the world in the guts and fight back. Have you got that moral courage, Mary? To me, you were a normal, happy-go-lucky young woman, up to the few weeks ago when you tragically went into that awful place and gave up the ghost. Why may I ask, did you wait for nearly 23 years and significantly until you went into that no hope place, to tell me that I was a failure as a father? You could have written it or spoken up years ago and damn well you know it.

As regards Mammy and I not being strictly honest with each other, I have not the foggiest idea what you are trying to get at except perhaps to try and sow trouble between us which I assure you, you or anyone else will never ever do. Mammy and I now love each other and depend on and trust each other far more than we ever did; thank god our love has matured with the years. We have gone through too much together for it to be otherwise. Marriage is not just a licence for cheap sex but a mutual agreement of love, respect, honour and trust (do you know anything of such things?) and mutual attraction and sex is just a very small integral necessary part of it. I prefer to call it mutual attraction as any cheap grotty whore can have sex at its cheapest and dirtiest, just like a pig in a farmyard muck or a mangy tom cat in an alley. Nothing you can ever say or do to your damdest will ever change my love for your beloved mother, god bless her and her huge generous heart in every way.

Speaking of your mother (I doubt if you care, as you seem to have become so insensitive to other people's pain, anguish and love), the unfortunate woman is living in a sort of dazed nightmare since you started your depredations. Some of the time she says nothing and sits as if dazed or in shock, or working herself to the point of cracking from exhaustion, trying to sleep at night which she just can't do and red-eyed, pale and wan from crying the rest of the time. All home-life is gone as the two boys are silent and look bewildered at what is happening, all because you have not the moral courage to face up to life, and kick it in the guts. If you think I am exaggerating, just come down here for one hour and see the appalling results of your cowardice, but remember, Mary, there is a just god in heaven and I know he will exact a terrible retribution on you for what you have done. Your mother is on tablets and is even giving concern to others and if she does not improve, she will have to go into hospital, all of which may give you no cause for concern – if it does not, Mary, all I can say is god have mercy on your immortal soul. I am being deadly calm now when I tell you that if as a result of your depredations that anything happens to your mother physically or mentally, I give you a solemn oath and promise that to my dying day I shall follow you to the very ends of the earth and make you pay a thousand times over for the agony and misery you have caused her, god help her, at this stage of her life. For your sake, I hope and pray it all never comes to that.

So, Mary, I am sure even you can see (you can't be that selfish and heartless) that something drastic will have to be done
before it gets too late. As you are always so fond of telling me,
you are free, white and twenty-one (I'm not so sure about being
free), but in any event you must have enough sense to realize
only too well that in the appalling environment of that ghoulish
hellhole where you are now that it will eventually kill you
morally, physically and mentally. You may vehemently protest
as much as you like to the contrary because it is a new and very
dangerous toy for you to play with and you can quote me your
dog-eared book until you are blue in the face and I would still
only scoff at such cheap and utter rubbish (the devil himself can
cite scripture for his purposes), but the plain honest fact is that
it will eventually warp your mind, apart from the obvious fact
you can't even hope to live in a normal decent human way in
such demoralizing surroundings, no matter what cheap excuses
you throw up to justify it. It is not only appalling, it is deadly
dangerous as well both to your mind and body and certainly
cannot and will not ever answer your problems. Very predictably, the day we went up there and went to such pains to meet
our own daughter, the pasty-faced Cockney one acted most
predictably when he attacked us like a madman (verbally of
course, because if he had laid a hand on me, he would have
been a hospital case), when I a mere normal mortal dared to
criticize the sick obscene daubings the whole way up the stairs
in that hellhole. The mere fact that he got so angry surely speaks
for itself and the idiotic lie that he is trying to fool himself into
believing is living; no matter what glossy sleazy cover or cloak
they try to put on the 'love and peace brother and sister' bit,
it is just plain and simple the haven of deadbeats and dropouts
and failures and a licence granted by themselves to wallow in
the filth and degradation of carnal animal lust.

How can any sane (I hope) intelligent normal girl be so
utterly naive and stupidly innocent or even dare to try and
justify such animal conduct. When you have gone (as you so
crudely put it) for love (do you mean lust) to other men, that

by the wildest stretch of the imagination is not love. It is just making an excuse to satisfy one's carnal animal passions and cheap lust. I grant you when he is defiling and degrading your unfortunate body and crawling all over you and panting like a slimy toad, he will undoubtedly whisper his idiotic gibberish and rubbish and meaningless muck to you; but when he has satisfied his animal appetites and sweaty dirty carnal lust, he will most surely throw you aside when he has bored of you, just as he has done to lots of other unfortunate young women, cast you aside Mary, like an old shoe or a dirty beer bottle and you will not be nor can you ever be even in the slightest bit happier because of such a degrading experience. Of course you must be well aware by now that a good deal of your fellow travellers and tragic misfits are European according to the police and only god knows how many dirty sweaty beds they have crawled out of right across Europe, leaving behind them a trail of human flotsam who turn into insane human cabbages, and go merrily on their way spreading and preaching their sick nonsense just as long as they can satisfy their animal sweaty lust. How, may I ask, would you feel if a daughter of yours wound up in such a place or if she found out her mother had once been in such a place? And then you have the gall to talk about having children when you are married who will have no 'hang-ups'. Your brothers are so angry at the downright misery you have caused that they would surely tell your kids anyway what sort of a mother you really are – they both have been told *everything* about you.

Then Mary, facts being facts, there is always the ever-present danger of venereal disease and syphilis, no matter how careful one tries to be in such circumstances. Have you ever seen anyone with VD, Mary? I have, during the war in the army where there was a special hut isolated to keep these unfortunates in as they slowly died and rotted away in appalling pain. The treatment, which never fully cures it, is extremely painful and the screams I have heard coming from that army hut would make even the most hardened shudder – what a pity you have not heard or seen it. Don't take my word for it – get a book and read about it for yourself. You can get VD from even a dirty toilet seat or even a cracked cup. Read about tough hard cases dying from VD going slowly blind and insane as foul-smelling sores and boils cover their genitals and private parts and spread to their intestines which rot away so that even going to the toilet is pure agony. I have heard of a case myself in that army hut where a fellow begged to die and made several attempts to kill himself. The children of such VD unions or marriages (if one can call it that) god help us, grow up deformed, mentally deficient, etc. Mary, I am asking you sanely and sensibly and in deadly calm – is that what you want out of life? You can go ahead and laugh and sneer all you want, and even delude yourself and quote all you want but as sure as day and night, what you are doing now will surely lead you to tragedy. Nature has an awful habit of kicking back – nothing is surer than that. I won't influence you in any way – I can't, but if it happens (god forbid!) you can't ever say I did not warn you. So go right ahead Mary and learn about life the hard way.

Since you have chosen this horrible way of life, I must now speak very bluntly to you on another topic. I was surprised and shocked last time you were home to find among your possessions a book on Lesbianism, but I told myself that it must be just idle curiosity; but the way things have now turned out, I am really worried and indeed disgusted. I hope and pray to god, Mary, that for your own sake and the sake of your family you are not dabbling in such appalling filth, because if you are (god forbid), you may as well be dead right now. This is the worst of all (my god, I must be losing my reason that I should have to even discuss such dirt with my own daughter) and the most degrading filth of all and leads to suicide or insanity. I hope and pray to god that you are not guilty of such a terrible thing but if it even crosses your mind in an ill hour, for god's sake, I beg of you please go straight to a doctor and get the proper treatment before it is too late, because what that will do to your mind and body is too terrible to even contemplate. The consequences of such a debauched life always show up in the face. Do you want to look like a riddled old hag even though you are still young?

Can you get it into your stupid head (now blinded by un-necessary hate and anger) what you are doing to yourself in such a place? It is *definitely not* the answer to yourself and will surely bring only more depression and black despair so before it gets too late and you are in too deep, pull out of it for god's sake. You must know in your heart of hearts that what you are doing will never or can never answer your problems and you will only get more depressed and bitter as time goes on and the novelty of that dreadful place wears off. It is summer now, Mary, and everything is lovely or so you think, but wait until winter comes with its long cold lonely wet nights and you are smothered with a cold or 'flu or worse, just see how your 'peace and love' brigade treat you then. Remember too, there is a very thin and delicate border between sanity and the awful alterna-tive and be very careful what you read and what is preached to you – it is highly dangerous to tamper with the mind.

Remember, Mary, it is now all completely and entirely up to you. I can do no more. We may not hear from you ever again. It will hurt and sadden me – maybe that is what you want, but it will be harder on me as I have to keep up a front before your mother, but it will surely put her into an early grave. Maybe you even want murder on your hands.

It's all entirely up to you from now on. I am disappointed in you to say the least of it, as I thought you had more spunk and guts and fight in you. Wherever you go, there can be no peace in such a life. DON'T BE A MORAL COWARD.

Dad."

★   ★   ★

14th February, 1976
"Dear Miss James,

It has come to my notice that my son Patrick is about to visit Atlantis again. As you are aware, Patrick was a patient in Shenley Mental Hospital. I claimed him out, and as his guardian am responsible for his well-being and safety. When he went to Atlantis last year, he thought and persuaded me that it may be the answer to his problems, so I agreed without looking into your set-up, also if you had any legal qualifications about conducting therapy. Well, as you know, he arrived at your place quite a reasonable person and within one month you had made him a really upset person, also brainwashing him that his parents were his real and dangerous enemies. I should have got after you then about this situation, but being a tolerant person, I let it go hoping that you wouldn't have any more dealing with him. Actually when he came home, he was only fit for hospital, but we managed to pull along and after a while he started to improve. Now get this straight, you or your friends are to *have no more to do with him* or I will have to take legal action against you for interfering with my son against my wishes. You just played a confidence trick on a weak-minded person and at the moment I am considering with my lawyer taking legal action against you for recovery of at least £260 which you got off Patrick by what I consider nothing less than false pretences. I would like to know what qualifications you have to conduct a therapy course. I suggest to you that when you receive this letter, you immediately telegraph Patrick not to visit your place. I assure you this is no idle threat but your *one and last chance* to keep clear of Patrick.

Yours truly,
J. Mahoney

PS Even if I deemed your place suitable for Patrick, I would not allow him to go there at the moment on account of the present political situation between North and South. As you know, a southern accent and a R. Catholic is the password for assassination."

20th February, 1976

"Mr. Mahoney:

I have today received your threatening and ill-informed letter.

I have no intention whatever of refraining from contact with Patrick as long as he himself wants it. He is not a child in your care, nor is he a mental patient. He is a friend of mine, someone I care about very much indeed, and I would not dream of betraying him through responding to your empty threats.

Patrick did not arrive at Atlantis 'quite a reasonable person'. He was most unreasonable, and this is one of the things that endeared him to us immediately. I did not make him into a 'really upset person.' I helped him to be more open about the fact that he is very upset indeed, feeling himself inferior to practically everyone he meets. I did not brainwash Patrick: I helped him clear away a few cobwebs from his eyes. It is obvious that you are not very happy with the truths he is telling. I do not enjoy the harsh truths my own 13-year-old daughter tells me; and my own mother was most unhappy about the truths I told her.

No-one at Atlantis wanted Patrick to leave when he did. His therapy was hardly begun and we considered it very bad for him to leave at that time. I am quite happy for you to take the 'legal action' you mention and am extremely intrigued to discover what Irish law gives a father jurisdiction over a grown-up son in his mid-twenties. You describe your son as weak-minded. I do not find Patrick weak-minded. I find him sensitive, intelligent, talented, loving, far-seeing and extremely hurt; I intend to do everything in my power to help him whenever he asks me to.

It may surprise you to know that there are people willing to pay thousands of pounds for the kind of therapy we do at Atlantis. I suggest you read my book *Room To Breathe*. You will naturally not like or agree with what I have to say, but at

least you may then know a little more substantially who it is
you are addressing your threats to.

                          Yours sincerely,
                          Jenny James."

                        ★   ★   ★

"Dear Miss James,

First of all, I want to introduce myself. I am John Murray's
mother. Please excuse this writing-paper. I am writing during
my lunch-time at school and I find that I haven't got my writing
pad with me.

I suppose you are aware that John and another man came to
our home one evening. We are all trying to blot the memory of
that visit from our minds. To say that it was a terrible experience
for me is to put it mildly. I know you are a mother, so you can
imagine what it was like for me to have a son whom you love
shouting and roaring, 'I hate you, I hate you'. As he said it, he
kept glaring at me, but all he could see in my eyes was love and
pity and sorrow. When I cried, his companion said, 'She is trying to make a baby out of you again.' Then when I spoke sharply
to him and told him to stop, his companion said, 'She is rejecting you now.' Both accusations of course were false. I never
treated John like a baby, except of course when he was a baby,
and then he was surrounded with love, security and all the other
things that I am sure you give your children. As for rejection,
it has never entered into my relationship with any of my children.
I wish you could know all about his background, but it would
take too long for me to tell you about it. Anyway, he can tell
you himself, that is if he is not already incapable of straight
thinking. I thought I gave him everything a child could need:
love, care, security, happiness, birthday presents and the hap-
piest Christmases any child could wish for. Then when he grew
older, he had in addition to that his books and his music which
he loved. Now it is very heart-breaking for me to find out that
he has found me wanting and hates me. I am trying to tell him
through you that everything I did for him was done with the

best of intentions. He always came to me when he wanted anything and I never let him down. I tried to talk to him, but he wouldn't communicate with me the way he should have done. He was always very shy and I feel that when he grew up, he should have made more of an effort to rid himself of that shyness. His brother and sister were reared in the same home and they have no difficulty in relating to people. I think he went to Atlantis to try to rid himself of his shyness, but feeding himself with anger and hatred will not help him. All that shouting will destroy his lungs and bronchial tubes. It is terrible to think that he has been screaming for the past two months. Where will it all end? I think the man that was with him was no help at all. I regret that I haven't got a tape-recording of the things he said. He spoke as if my husband and I had set out all our lives with one object in view, that is, of destroying and rejecting our son, which of course is completely and utterly false.

I am appealing to you to undo any harm that has been done. If you have any influence over them, let God into their lives. God means love, not hatred and anger against people who do not deserve it. I hope you will remind John of last Christmas when he came to me and did not find we wanting. As soon as he comes to me again with love, I will be there as I have always been. If you think my husband and I can help him in any way, will you kindly let us know.

I hope I have not taken up too much of your time. Kiss your children for me. Christmas is such a happy time for them. I hope it will be happy for you too and for John and for all at Atlantis. When Jesus will knock at your door, I hope there will be room for Him.

Very sincerely,
Mrs. Murray."

29th December, 1976
"To: Mrs. Murray,

I did know that John and a friend went down to your house, but I knew no details other than that you had called the police to have them ejected.

With regard to John's upbringing, I know very little at all, simply because he does not speak. The idea of him 'screaming' for two months is quite astonishing to me. It would delight us to hear any kind of loud noise issuing from your son, but it does not happen. I can tell you that John is so far the most repressed Irish person of the dozens who have come to us; he himself does not know how he got like this, as he believes you were kind to him.

You talk to me a lot about god, but you are talking to a complete atheist. I find the Catholic religion and what it does to the children in Ireland quite evil. I find the beatings doled out by the Christian Brothers and other teachers and parents horrific, though I understand from every Irish person who comes to me that such treatment is completely 'normal' over here. I could not possibly recommend your god to John.

I am not able to offer you any of the reassurance that you ask for since your position is one of outraged innocence and piety, whereas my only concern is to see John find his manhood, power and strength and not to continue wafting around as if in a dream with no energy or autonomy of his own.

You ask what you and your husband could do to help John. The only thing I can think of is to take his difficulties seriously and not keep throwing love and caring in his face when he attempts to voice what he feels. It is rather ironic that the minute he finds some strength, you call the authorities to shut him up once more. That doesn't sound like love to me.

Yours sincerely,

Jenny James."

1977

ATLANTIS YEAR THREE: AUTUMN

I used to believe that I never learnt a single useful thing in my three years at London University.

Then the other day I remembered a young Welsh anarchist in the first year telling me, 'Even if I was falling to my death from the top of a skyscraper, I'd make sure I went with one hell of a SPLAT!'

I quietly dismissed him as mad. But somehow his words stuck in my head. Ten years later, I know what he meant.

Enlightenment comes from strange sources.

So I did learn one thing in my three years at university after all.

9th November, 1977

★   ★   ★

AUTUMN is a sad, beautiful, wistful, nostalgic, lonely, weather-beaten, ripe time; a time when all illusions are stripped: when there is only the stark reality of the harvested earth, the tragic colourfulness of dying leaves. It is a haunting time, a time of longings and wonderings; a time of endings and tyings-up and completions. The exuberance, enthusiasm and youthfulness of Starting has gone; the wisdom, quietness, sadness, strength and resolve of Having Seen remain.

So with Year Three of Atlantis. If Year One was Atlantis Introverted, and Year Two Atlantis Made Public, Year Three was the both together: dealing with our internal pains and fears and needs in the face of incredibly strong forces from within and without intent on battering us down. Anyone who felt touched, affected, disturbed by us and didn't admit it, simply wanted us off the face of the planet – especially the 'left-wing' in the form of squatting activists around our London base and the 'pacifist' fortnightly *Peace News* who chose to print an even more absurd and paranoid 'display' of Atlantis than the *Sunday World* had done – and like the *Sunday World,* without even bothering to send a reporter round. Those of us seasoned in the struggle were still vaguely amazed at these reactions. We had to learn

once again that people really are just people, with all their
magnificence and all their nonsense. They are not 'left', 'right'
or any other label, just irrational beings lashing out blindly when
made uncomfortable. The unclassifiability of Atlantis brought
out the peopleness in people everywhere! All boundaries and
barriers were turned topsy-turvy. Some of the main 'street
leaders' in our road of squats in London crossed the street,
dropped their prejudices, chose a mate, and joined us: this
caused eruptions, as we were supposed to be the 'crazies', the
'non-politicals', the ones with all the taboo concepts and unacceptable behaviour (and leftwingers are incredibly conventional).
If some of their best men were attracted to our colour and
exuberance, then perhaps we weren't so dismissible after all!

I just love our effects! I love the fact that Mick, a handsome,
semi-literate heavy-drinking IRA man from Northern Ireland
falls crazily in love with us – with our women in particular of
course – and in spite of every possible cultural, political, class
and personal barrier ends up living with us at Atlantis on
Inishfree Island, giving up the booze, telling us of his previous
unhappiness, and entering into the depth of life's stream as never
before. I purr at the thought that Pete, everyone's bouncer and
bully-boy, could feel our spirit and spark sufficiently through
all his drugs and alcohol and preconceived notions to walk
softly into our kitchens at long last, shy, proud, but with ears,
eyes and heart open. I love it that there is no 'protectionism' in
our tribe: that people who want to lean and cower and mope
and drip all over us are heartily termed 'wankers' (there are
plenty of the female sort too) and kicked out or laughed out.
I love it that we are not 'safe'. We do not keep ourselves safe
and we do not keep each other safe. The only security is truth:
At Atlantis, 'Reality Rules OK!' There is no artificial comrade-
ship, loyalty or honour: we are not a club, a movement or a
group. It's painful, it's lonely at times, it's always enlightening.
But when love and warmth come, when praise or appreciation
are given, they are red-hot real, and no shoddy goods.

So, in this chapter – fights with the Outside; struggle on the inside; love, viciousness, fear, beauty and fun . . .

One of the dangers of pushing things all the way with people is what they do with their bad feelings when they block and leave our communes. As predictable as sunrise, their fury at being made to face themselves comes back at us in some under- hand way, either aimed at the community as a whole or at whichever individual within it has affected them most deeply. Such comeback varies from slander articles in the press to threats of actual physical violence. In January 1977, in a road of 'leftwing' squats, I was threatened by a guy I'd never met before who claimed to be a karate expert willing to kill. He had evi- dently appointed himself protector of a girl who had been asked to leave our London commune. The girl, peeved at being thrown out, had managed to convince people in the area that she needed protection from the dreaded Screamers. We were furious at what she was doing, but were prevented from having it out with her face to face. I decided to blow the whole situation wide open by allowing a letter I'd written her to be circulated to the whole street of squats. I knew I was in danger, but I felt it was worth it – better anyway to bring things to a head than live in an atmos- phere of hypocrisy and paranoia. Here is an excerpt from the letter. It certainly blew things open!

4th January, 1977
Here is a letter for you to feed on for the next couple of years. Just think, Mary, the glory of it, *you* actually know from inside the full horror of the dreaded Screamer communes: only you can reveal the full story in all its gory detail from personal experience and suffering (and oh my god how you have suffered, poor innocent angel). And what is more, you'll be able to provide a Service by reassuring everyone that they are Not Missing Anything, no, life is just as they always thought, mean and devious and cunning, to be worked out, thought out, handled with care, planned and plotted, motives to be sought, people to be held at a distance (you can't trust anyone these days). Yes,

these people need you, a fine enlightened young woman, they need you to comfort them in their mediocrity and boredom: don't worry, you can tell them, YOU'RE NOT MISSING ANYTHING, really, this is all life is, just a titillation here, a little zing there, a little thrill and then quick! retract, recoil, go back, for after all, it's nasty out there, dangerous, and we mustn't let too much out, must we? Those illusioned people down the road like Jenny James and her crew, they just think they know something different, but they're mad, don't worry friends, really, they have nothing for you to be jealous of, just keep away from them, they're dangerous. They are particularly dangerous because they have this nasty unfair non-British habit of making you feel, of making you see things you don't want to see, and that is very inconvenient, for it causes you to have to use a lot of energy to pull down the shutters even tighter, a lot of spaghetti-brain energy to work out ways of counteracting all those nasty feelings that keep surging up.

Still, chin up friends, it's easy really, just look: we are in the vast majority, why everyone agrees with us, the press and the police and everyone in this nice leftwing liberal alternative squatting road, all the lovely protective people who listen to me for hours on boring end while I tell all my exciting stories and all the terrible things they did to me and I so poor and hurt and confused. And look! here comes sweet free-flowing red-cheeked Blumchen to confirm all my tales – look, they have broken up her perfect marriage and lured her loyal husband away – now do you see! Oh what triumph! now you can all see how right I am, how there is nothing wrong with me at all, fatness is just individuality and pimples are natural and myopia is simply a medical condition, and confusion of the brain is congenital and perfectly livable-with; no, there is nothing twisted about me at all.

Oh, but what is this? That nice Clive, whom I thought I had completely under my wing – damn it! He slipped out when I wasn't noticing and started doing unpredictable things. But I can explain it! See how clever my spaghetti-brain is. CLIVE

HAS BEEN TAKEN OVER. That's it! I knew there was a reason why he wouldn't prefer my exciting company to those mad women up the road. Yes, that's it, he's been hypnotized, mesmerized, he doesn't know his own mind, he's not being himself – yes, that's a good one, that'll get to him (that's the one my parents used on me, so I know it works really well – you're not quite yourself today Mary, you were all right before you went to That Place).

Oh dear, oh dear, I still don't feel satisfied, how can that be? I have comfort and karate and control at my fingertips. I have all any sensible girl could wish for, I have cleverness and I have that which I have always secretly most longed for: Power and Violence on my side; and still, damn it, there is something eating at me, a nasty feely-weely I thought I'd got rid of.

Could it be, oh no, surely not, it can't be . . . something missing? Emptiness? Hollowness? NO, DEFINITELY NOT. I will fill it up, see, I'll get money, I'll get more people listening to me, I have more and more dreadful troubles to tell – look what this nasty woman is doing now writing nasty letters to me! How dare she, she thinks she can do anything. I'll show her. Now, how can I get at her this time without making too much noise, without taking any risks, without making myself vulnerable, without finding my legs, without feeling my true strength, without getting to know myself, without feeling anything uncomfortable? Now let me see, how can I get out my murderous strangling gollumish violence this time, now let me see . . . I'll work out something.

Ah yes! of course, I'd nearly forgotten. Why, it's simple! It's them who are violent, obviously! Yon can see it, you can hear it – everyone's heard it already, everyone knows about the nasty screamers. Of course! Hear ye all, *they're* the violent ones. Look! I'm just a little marshmallow dumpling, tiny dainty hands and little feet, a tiny mouth that nothing Big could ever possibly come out of; soft little baby muscles that have never been used for anything heavier than pouring cups of tea – I am so proud of the fact that I can't even light a fire you know –

gentle femininity and helplessness just oozes out of me all over
the place; that is why big brave hard men just longing to kill,
kill for me you see. I am the eternal helpless little girl, why even
the women's libbers are fooled by me, for I talk a lot, and that
is Intellectual you know, and they just love that. Oh, I have
something for everyone; everyone that has something to hide
that is.

Now that's the trouble with these nasty screamy shouty people:
they don't hide anything. And that creates a problem. For I
feed on people's fears. These damn brazen people are difficult.
But of course it'll be their downfall, because it's so easy to get
at them. They just lay themselves open. I can't understand their
stupidity at all, they're really naive, they do so many illegal and
unacceptable and provocative things, why I can get at them
from left, right and centre. It's so easy, so pathetically easy, to
prove they are the violent ones. I just have to snivel and grovel
and weep and yap – a little snipey weepy word here and wham!
that nasty Jenny turns into a volcano; a clever little twisty here
and pow! reasonable Bernard turns into a fishwife and slaps
me – just like I'd love to slap him, the nasty clever heady
bastard, he can almost beat me at my own game; but I've got
him now, why it's clear that he's a terrifying bully, because I had
to hide away from him for days on end and I needed dozens of
people to protect me from him, for I was *confused* you see, and
needed time to plan, I mean think, and so all my nice new gentle
friends protected me so that that nasty Bernard wouldn't say
anything to me that would get at me, that would bring up those
feelie weelies I have so preciously under control. It was really
lucky for me that my nice new friends had a little private hoard
of shit for Bernard themselves, otherwise they might have
noticed that he is rather small and skinny and that I could have
socked him right over. But whew, the gamble came off, a few
tears and frightened looks and everyone could see that he is a
six-foot bully and that I need protection from the whole street.

I am a bit worried now though, because I'm not sure how
long I can keep this up. I mean – won't they get bored with me,

once the novelty has worn off? I mean, I wonder how long I can keep them fed with excitement to get off on? Oh dear, I wonder what I shall do then, because these nasty therapy people that I used to go to with all my moans, they lost patience with me and stopped being nice to me, and stopped giving me cups of tea and Christmas cake, and started telling me the horridest things about myself . . . and just when I'd trusted them too, just when I found this lovely Therapy where I could be weak and moan for the rest of my cushioned days, just when I thought all my dreams of getting looked after and appreciated had come true; suddenly this nasty Jenny woman and all her friends turn round and tell me to get off my arse, flex my muscles, wobble my jelly around a bit and start to be robust – horrid word – instead of effete and delicate. And when I explain to them at great and complicated length why I can't move or answer back and why it is absolutely essential to my well-being to spend the rest of my days cooking plum puddings and nattering breezily over friendly cups of tea, why those horrid monsters who promised to look after me (that's what Therapy is for, isn't it?), they get really annoyed, and then they say all sorts of unflattering things to me, and then, to cap it all, they say they don't trust me, can you imagine it, me perfect little angel, they say they don't trust my meekness and sweetness and sugar and spice, why they say they think it's violent of me to absorb all their nasty comments and sit on them, and I just can't understand it, but they get angrier and angrier with me instead of being nice to me and sympathetic to me in my confusion, and then, finally, they say they cannot stand to live with me any more; they say strange cultish things like I'm 'draining their energy' and 'spreading unreality around the kitchen,' and they say awful things like they feel like strangling me – just because I'm a sweet innocent soft confused little girl; they say perhaps that would help me out of my confusion? That's how violent and nasty and intolerant those horrid therapy people are.

But I'll show them! I'll teach them what happens when people refuse to see my talent, my beauty, my intelligence, my vast superiority; I'll teach them to put me down, I'll show them what happens when they try messing with the cushionings of a nice average loving British family background like mine, all those friendly Christmas cakes – why my granddad even visited me at the therapy commune, that's what a loving family I come from. I'll show them a thing or two about the ways of the world, those silly naive therapy people who thought I really wanted to come alive; I wouldn't be so stupid. I just wanted a little sympathy, that's all.

And that's what I've got now. A little sympathy. That's all.

4th January, 1977
"Dear Jill,

I am kneeling down with restricted breathing to write to you.

It may be that the black cloud has passed and gone, but much more likely there is more and worse to come. Just like in *Lord of the Rings,* there are resting places, havens of peace, moments of humour even – like when Becky, knocking at a door to try to speak to Mary, found herself face-to-face with Mr. Karate himself, and so went to knock at the next door – to be faced with him again. The houses have been joined inside. Moments of mirth too when we held a group in occupied territory – in Mary's house. We stayed there so that she'd have to face us instead of using other people to do her dirty work. But we left after twenty-four hours and ended the siege; another minute bothering about her would have bored us to tears.

At times, I wonder if my judgment is intact. Sometimes I am shaken by the dithering of others, swayed and blown myself, and then I doubt; am I inventing all the murder and blackness and danger that surrounds us? Is it really as people say, that we are the violent ones, that shouting is violent and self-control kind? That Mary is Weak?

And then I find myself again of course. But in the fear and pain of the night, there is a dagger in my stomach churning and turning, twisting, keeping me awake and unbreathing with pain. And then in the morning, I get up to get sessions together and the wintry sun is shining and the street seems normal and energy moves in me and my night pains are gone. But the doubting will come back again; I can slip so easily, just like anyone else. I need to write to you in order to get my intactness and life-flow back, in order to see what it is that torments me when I am alone with my thoughts. There is so much evil around, so much twisted life-force, that it is a terrible struggle to stay feeling as well as thinking clearly so that the mechanized daleks don't win. Reich saw it all and went mad on it in the end, it was too much for him, because he didn't have a group around him strong enough to fight the blackness in him.

These days are so full and busy; this war is intense. A psychiatrist would say I'm mad: where's the war? Where are the weapons? Where's the enemy? You're hallucinating, you're paranoid. There's just sweet ineffectual little Mary peering from behind spectacles having a weep or two, ranting on in circles, obviously confused and harmless and needing protection quite understandably from karate freaks who believe in violence but not in shouting your truth at one another; who switch on full-beam Control or I'll kill you if your flesh moves or shivers or if you make blood move in my veins.

The sun is shining on this paper, my guts are starting to ache and that's good. I'm moving. If you don't see me again, good-bye! I love you all, and I'm scared.

Jen."

5th January, 1977
"To the Folks Back Home:

Today is the first quiet day. I don't know how long it will stay like this. I'm tired of fighting, I feel depressed and low. I have been so highly geared to cope with what's happening in the street, that now it's all quietened down, my energy is adrift.

I am full of hatred at the moment for the weak men in our commune, and my feeling grows when I meet people like Pete, the street 'bouncer' who came to ask me to leave the street and whom all our men are scared of. But I'm not! I like him; he is punchdrunk and crazy, lashing out all over the place, sneering and dismissive and terrorizing everyone. And yet when he came to persuade me to go, I had more fun with him in half an hour than with our menfolk in months. He's awful, but he is playable-with; I prefer his chaotic stroppiness and defensiveness to the dead soggy sensible lumps that come to us for 'help'. I am seeing more and more how people don't change at all through therapy: as they begin, so they continue. It's just that more and more of them shows. All the seeds are there the first day. 'Therapy' of course is just a beautiful alive open environment where you can flower if you want to and where people won't like you if you don't! Now that I've thoroughly dropped my care-taking attitude, I think the cosmic vibe we're sending out will attract fewer and fewer primal twits and more and more real live gutsy human beings.

My own growth in seeing is so slow; it was my own haziness that allowed Mary to spend six months grotting at Atlantis: we should have thrown her out after a week. I've learnt loads from you, Jill; I feel you brought your own brand of health to Atlantis; you came as a doer instead of a sucker.

My Mary letter caused lots of trouble in the street which ambassadors from here did their best to turn to good contact. Andy messed the whole thing up by posting copies of it through the doors anonymously instead of relating to people over what I had written. One of our fellows was knocked over and punched in the jaw by Pete the Bouncer for speaking back to him. There were about ten of Pete's 'friends' sitting around pretending nothing was happening. Weirdly enough, I had a session about Pete today and I just cried and cried about him. I see him as a big bruised King Kong whom no-one sees and everyone uses or hates or is frightened of. I'm really going to try to get through to him. He does disgusting things all the time, but I'm not going to join in the chorus of 'he's a jolly bad fellow' any more than I'd ever be part of his group of 'friends' who never challenge him because they're shit-scared of him turning on them.

So the barriers are blurring in this street! I am not on the side

of the 'therapy house', though no-one on the other side of the
street would know it or believe it if they were told, for I am the
'coven leader' according to Pete himself. Yesterday evening,
when I was in the loo, I heard a fight in our hallway. It turned
out that Pete had called round to see me, and Graham had
jumped on him because Pete, as usual, had sneeringly put him
down. Even so, I felt bad about it happening here on our territory where it was safe, and even worse, Andy joined in and
loads of our people were crowding round. I thought that was
disgusting, and I ended up hating all our men's guts even more
and I went round to see Pete and communicate with him. But he
came to his door drunk and stoned and hurt and freaked out,
ready for a fight and holding a bottle behind his back. I still
didn't feel scared of him at all. I feel more frightened of the
crying and hurt he brings up in me.

Every time I challenge our men on why they are so
'frightened' of him, it always turns out that it's their own
violence they are scared of – scared of how much he makes them
want to kill with his cutting sarcasm and dismissiveness. I know
for sure that anyone who is genuinely frightened acts tough and
fierce to counteract it; the cowering meek submissive people are
always the real killers.

So JJ, 'female Charles Manson' as Pete has called me behind
my back (whilst also admitting that he 'likes my spirit'), turns
out to be defender of the strong, judge of the pseudo-meek, and
anti-therapy champion; and who knows what tomorrow may
hold. I might try learning a bit of karate myself, or simply continue relying on my big mouth which seems to be serving me
quite well at present!

I've cheered up considerably just writing this letter, it's
tumbling out in a jumble, but my energy has returned and things
don't seem so flat now. I'm still little miss scaredy-cat, fear is
with me all the time, fear of being hated and mis-seen. That is
the great anxiety that never leaves me. I have no fear of being
hit, just the ever-present danger of being hated to death. I am
scared of walking out of the front door and down the street,

terrified of going to other people's houses; even when Becky
was sleeping with Mike across the street, I was stricken with
fear when calling for her. But when I do actually talk to people,
I enjoy it enormously. It seems I happily play into people's
image of me as the evil, powerful baddy, I'm so used to that.
Suddenly, I realize why I was crying so bitterly about Pete in
my session today – that's what he does, of course, plays baddy
for both sides; he never pretends to be good like the really evil
ones.

    Well, I'll end now as obviously I must go off into the Great
Outside to encounter Pete some more.

                                        Shivers and love, Jenny."

12th January, 1977
"Dear Jill,

    On this beautiful and sad and scary morning, I have read your
huge report on the state of darkness and light at Atlantis and
I have cried in sorrow. The news you send of Oisin hurts a lot,
because it makes me realize I do need him to come through;
I do still hope and believe that he cannot wipe out all he has
learnt and seen and been through. I suppose I need to believe
in the ultimate good of man, to believe that good is stronger
than evil. I need to believe that the beauty and life in Oisin will
triumph. But I also realize that I haven't learnt half my lesson
about human beings. My training continues. I still have to understand the evil that is tapped in so many people just through us
expressing our good life energy. I don't want to end up with
some theory that there are 'two sorts of people', that God and
Devil are incarnate in separate beings. I want to see someone
who has been completely Black become completely White and
never ever use the pit of impotence again. I can't think of anyone I've seen this happen to. So many people revel in 'moments
of light' but always keep open a sneaky little return-exit back
to the darkness when life gets too hot and bright – so many
people I've known have really 'seen' and really 'been' and yet
they've always kept that Gollumish cleverness, always kept a

little black corner to crawl back into, never really opened and
made themselves completely vulnerable to life energy. It is quite
terrifying to me how few people care for life itself over and
above all else, above all personal survival, all danger and punishment. Once people you are working with have really 'seen', Jill,
and then stepped backwards deliberately, you should chuck
them out to choose between life and death somewhere else. Your
letter has made me more obsessed than ever with our power or
inability to do something about the way life is being twisted on
this planet. I feel speed is really important. I've always attempted
to hold back my own speed, which is my strength, because I
feared no-one could keep up with me and I'd be left alone.
But I just have to speed on; that is my reality. My speed is my
power to bring life to others. WE MUST BE QUICK: this is
my message, this is the message of my body, of my energy, of
my pain and fear, we must be quick, and I am going to be
quick; let anyone who feels my own urgency join in, overtake,
pull me along; and those who can't stand me for it, counteract
me. I feel headachey and breathless through restricting my own
speed. People call me speedy and impatient; and yet I am curb-
ing my real speed because I desperately need others to speed
along with me or to slow me down with some alternative loving
power of their own, but never to stop me dead with deadness.
I have been hated to death for my speed, but my speed is my
life because I AM THE SLOWEST OF YOU ALL. I took the
longest to see. I hovered around in that other world the longest.
I put up with getting nothing the longest. I took the longest to
notice there was something very wrong. I was the last to learn
to live, and I will be the first to die."

20th February, 1977
"Jerry,
    An attempt at communication; I want to tell you what life is
like for me now and where I have got to after the holocausts
that everyone went through last autumn at Atlantis.

I reached just a step away from ecstasy on my island with my man, with my goats and the wild Atlantic. But I am only thirty-four and I was not allowed to rest yet, which is what I wanted to do, to grow into the soil and stay on the peatbogs forever. To do that, I felt I needed Oisin, but he was not ready; he had to travel to Mordor, he's gone there and I don't know if he'll ever come back. I was ready for embroidery and rocking-chairs and illiteracy and children born wild and free, but it was not to be and I had to break my heart-strings and move on again. I had dreamed of retiring, but I get the feeling some energy force is organizing my place on this planet and it was telling me: 'There is more work to be done'; not the easy work of carrying wood and water and milking the goats and nursing baby chicks; I had to return to the city once more.

So I have come here to make some discoveries, and the first discovery I have made is that clairvoyance is real. I came looking for a new kind of person to join us, especially people who are into the occult. Before I left Eire, I found some witches who may have much to teach. You chose to go East, Jerry, but there is Celtic magic under very ordinary-looking stones if you care to turn them with love – maybe you will let me take you West one day, just for fun?

I want to travel now further into the stars, into the palms of my hands and into discovering whether or not the spirit of my parents still walks and stalks; I intend to talk to them through mediums to find out. And one day, I am bound for America to see how our Atlantean experience tallies with that of others who have gone far.

I learnt so much this autumn – that true exorcism has nothing to do with noise or the cushion-bashing of early therapy days. Few go through the deepest horrors voluntarily, though those who really want to live, face the terror of their own power more willingly than others. I am a pusher, and I believe it is right to push. This is not a game or a palliative or some groovy experiment or middle-class alternative-to-aspirin. This is a cosmic revolution we are taking part in.

I want to tell you about some extraordinary black things that have surged up from the depths of people at Atlantis through our deep digging. I never knew of the existence of such things except perhaps from Tolkien; I never guessed at their reality except through tales of concentration camps; I've never seen them mentioned in psychology books except in the form of Reich's 'Deadly Orgone Radiation,' 'emotional plague' and 'death layer.' It is what comes out when you keep pushing and don't accept the excuse 'I'm stuck.' It is what happens when you don't compromise, but take it to the limit. And beyond. It is what comes out of people when they are challenged and pushed and fought and forced instead of being allowed to find solace in gossip and private nasty thoughts and bemoaned frustrations.

What I have seen at Atlantis is person after person turn temporarily into insane befanged monsters with hideous electrifying eyes; it happens under guidance of course, and sometimes after days and weeks of heavy pushing. We have a sense for it now; we know when some enormous subterranean force has to come out. When there is a white or green or grey deathly palour to the skin, when the person has gone dead and limp and meek, sure enough if you push, out will come the pet family monster. No-one can fake: no-one can pretend to be going through it. There is a very special something in the whites of the eyes that chills your spine and electrifies everyone in the room when the person is truly contacting his devils, and always, always – to my amazement, but so obvious really – the person goes through feelings of flesh-tearing and eating. Can you imagine sweet Pepe, grey as death with bulging eyes and teeth growing longer, sweating and straining at the leash, wanting to kill – his daughter? Because she was crying for him. And Oisin, well, the murder in him was always pretty near the surface. He electrified a whole room as we hauled his father to the surface in him, forcing him to look in a mirror and see just who was living inside him. There was beauty and love in the horror as one by one, silently, for hours on end, a shift-service of shocked but reverent Atlanteans held the mirror up for him as he went through it.

He chose to cut off afterwards, but he will have to go back to that point and regurgitate the whole of Ireland through his eyes and mouth if he wants to move onward.

Some people go in voluntarily, though horrified at showing all that hideous murderousness in their face. Gaby had to become a female Gollum, slowly, whisperingly catching and chewing up tiny babies as she felt her mother in her. She was forced to face this by us challenging her with how much of an 'accident' her own baby's death had been. I sat with her for hours while she went, naked and beautiful in her bravery, through her ugliness. The times I have had to become my own mother and show her madness in my eyes, I will leave to those who saw me to describe. Screaming is minor compared to this kind of energy. None of us was killed with free-flowing energy, and when the killing comes out, it is slow and calculated and spine-chilling."

★ ★ ★

March, 1977
"To a friend; on arriving home at Atlantis after spending the winter in London.
Dear John,

Your amazing letter came three days ago and I have not yet told you how shocked I was at the honesty you allowed yourself in it; I feel your seeing is so clear when you write about yourself and I completely respect you for knowing you cannot jump into boiling water 'being protected' by me; it has to be your own jump and your own water in your own time. I think you have gone further without 'going anywhere' than plenty of guys who come to therapy thinking they want to go places!

I hope you find your own way; though I still doubt whether you'll choose boiling water. These doors are open to you at any time in your life; I cannot offer to be your woman in them, but I can guarantee to you that it will always be an amazing and alarming place to be.

A few words about the praise and awe, and simple seeing too, that you give me in your letter. I want to tell you that although I appreciate your admiration, this is not what I need at all. It was once in my life years ago when I met with nothing but criticism for my way of being and working with people; but that is long ago now.

I want to tell you what I need from a man, and that is for him to make me feel completely small. I want someone who hasn't read my books, who doesn't know me, but who responds to me immediately as a challenge to be conquered; someone who doesn't want to run alongside me or sit worshipping me, or to stop my life-energy, but who simply wants to own me completely and make sure he makes his mark on me and on this place and who has a deep understanding of what power really is. I've been talking about it for years and so far it is mainly the women I know now who have understood what it's about. I want a man to come here and see what he knew always to be true put into practice at Atlantis; this will excite him and turn him on completely so that he will want to walk in here and take over immediately, with only the most formal of hesitations.

I feel I have been in the practice of true 'power' for years – and I know that is a negative word in nearly everyone's ears, for it has taken on such sinister meaning this century. But I see that you know what I mean when you talk of Gandalf. The man I want must be completely into his own power – and that means his body and passions first, for that way lies a clear intellect. Head in air without body fire is empty, that's what the western world is made of. Come and talk to me one day of these things on my thinking rock in Atlantis garden!

love, Jen."

Back in Brixton
2nd July, 1977
"Dear Anne and Chris,

I am in the sun of the garbage-dump garden of No. 13 Canterbury Crescent. I feel I have been transported by some

turn in the wheel of Fate back to this place. I am totally unhappy, but totally myself. Once again, I find myself a vehicle
of Movement – other people's; but also my own, because
although I am totally unhappy, there is that spot of white in the
blackness. I have myself and will be open and receptive when
good comes my way.

What is happening is that I find my tolerance for shit ever
lowering. At the moment, Gaby is full of shit, and I have had
to bust things up with her, or go down a slippery grey slope and
get lost in the murk. Becky, I am thinking of you now and how
let-down and angry you got with me when I lost myself with
Babs and didn't fight sufficiently. Well, I want to tell you that
now I am not selling out anywhere or with anyone and that as a
result, I am in raw pain and I need you to love me, because I
tell you, there aren't many people who love me for being who
I am. I feel violently angry at this moment with anyone who
goes weak and 'confused' and apologetic around me. I'm just
beginning to see how all my paleness and depression is me trying
to like what is coming into me when all my senses are rebelling
and telling me quite rightly that what's coming into me is Shit.

Everyone at the London commune has been shaken up by me
and I completely accept now that I am a Mover. I am dripping
sweat in this boiling sun and I'm starting to feel really good.
It is a relief not to be caught up in defending myself against
hatred by saying, 'Really, I'm not that big, I'm just little, I'll
keep my mouth shut, don't notice me please.'

I am a very belated developer: thirty-five and still obscenely
having long periods of feeling bad; I make myself sick. Well,
I promise myself here and now that I'll never have another
birthday like my last, wanting to die. This morning, I was convinced that I had to lose everyone, and yet as soon as I lose
everyone, all sorts of miraculous things happen. Please, any of
you who are preparing for any future sojourns in the pit of
murk, heed me and take warning: you *have* to lose everyone
before you gain yourself. What availeth it a woman if she
gaineth everyone by licking their arses and loseth the Queendom

of her own soul? Clare! If you don't open your mouth, you're already gone; Jill, if you don't do something radical to fight me, then we are already enemies. Anne, my leaving Atlantis at this point is the best thing that ever happened to you (except for you going there in the first place): you have eleven years advantage over me; use them well! Become the biggest most powerful witch, for when I come home, I want to take my rightful place – in the most comfortable back seat.

love, Jen."

Words from Patsy

"I want to tell you my dream.

We are having a group. Jenny is sitting separately. A vision of a woman appears, she is brilliant and shining and fair and white and just amazingly Good. Then suddenly, over her left shoulder, the most evil Thing appears; it is the most evil thing in the world. First, I'm seeing through Jenny's eyes. Then I see Jenny and she's turned black and her eyes are staring and she's not moving and at first I think she has turned evil, but then I see it's because she's seen evil and is horrified and paralysed by it. I have the most terrible feeling; people have to stay with Jenny all the time now in case she does something terrible – kill herself maybe. There are nuns everywhere and everything is dark and wooden. I look into the room where Jenny is being kept, a kind of cell, and I see it is just beginning to dawn. It is very beautiful. I think she must see that it is beautiful and that it will make her break through her horror. Suddenly, I hear her shriek and I run to her and she is even more horrified, and I can't see what is horrifying her except a few clouds on the left, but the rest is beautiful.

Then I'm cycling along and I can't stop thinking of her. I feel she has been like this for a long time. I'm trying to think of how I can get through to her and I'm planning to go and take her by the hand and just let whatever comes into my head come out. I wake up then and tell Mick the dream and I start crying. The room I am sleeping in with Mick is where I lived from the age of four to eighteen. It is where a lot of horrible things happened, where I was beaten up and where I used to lie on the bed and wish I was dead and then I used to take a deep breath, look out of the window and find something like a tree or a blue sky or sunset that would make me want to live.

I know that in the dream I am Jenny. I realized as I told the dream to Mick that I trust Jenny more than anyone in the world because she doesn't play games and she knows herself. Whenever I doubt myself or my own feelings, I go into her. She is my yardstick. It is me that is full of horror, stone cold and freezing, carrying it around all the time, and I could never let myself really feel a dawn or anything beautiful because the horror was always there – on the left, clouds on the left, my mother side; my mother and her insanity. All my life, I've wanted someone to come to me and tell me that it's all right, that I don't have to be scared any more.

And that's what the last year has been like for me, with you all. At every stage when someone has said to me some little commonsense thing about myself, like that I am weak inside, I think, 'Really? Is that OK then? Am I allowed? Can I dare?' And each time, I've sunk into myself a little more, relaxed a bit more and let myself know I don't have to be scared any more, so that now when I see a dawn (he's lying beside me now), I can let him in from the top of my head to my toes.

Mick and I are very happy. I find it amazingly easy to come now, even before Mick does, and I'm a very satisfied woman. I look back at all the years of horrible hurting sex. It was fear turned to hate and I would hurt because I didn't know where to begin to feel any of it. A prick was an instrument of torture because no matter how I tried – and I did try – I couldn't stop feeling. So sex was a struggle, all the time me fighting and strain-ing not to feel, but very luckily I didn't manage. There I was in the most acute pain pretending I was enjoying it because doesn't everyone? Now I know if I'd allowed myself all the feelings that were there at the time of making love, I would have just howled and howled with pain and fury.

Writing this is amazing. I'm seeing loads. I started out feeling quite bad from the dream, but I feel really good now.

                                                    love, Patsy."

Words from Pete Brind at Atlantis

"Dear Jenny,

Who are you? I'm not sure at all! There is a huge myth still surrounding you, in my eyes that is. I've been running away from myself for so long that it's hard to see other people at all; let alone allow them to know me.

I had my first 'session' today! It started in a group last night with Anne. She told me how she saw me. It frightened the shit out of me: a giant striding with his head in the clouds, floundering along without knowing that his head was separate from his body. It was like waking up into a bad dream. The realization that I have never allowed anyone into me, or allowed the me imprisoned out, was too incredible to let in till this morning. The weight of my years came crashing down on me. I felt old beyond words. Letting my body sink with my face, the pain of keeping the strong man façade was over for a time, letting the pretence ooze away.

I once said to you that I had an 'OK' relationship with my parents. I didn't realize what lies I'd been living under. I felt the way they'd 'sacrificed' for me, but how they'd never given me what I needed most – their love. I needed their time, but I never got it. I rebelled, but I was made to feel bad about letting them down. 'Even as a baby, Peter was always good, never cried.' As a teenager, up till Villa Road, I lived at a different pace, becoming a wraith speeding from here to there with the least possible contact. A few words here, a sentence there, not exposing myself, not risking rejection again.

Drugs were an easy way out. I did it to give me something they never did: warmth. But heroin makes you too sensitive to what people say, so take more to send you to sleep. Instead of fucking them over, I fucked myself over. My overdose was an attempt to end my loneliness, but luckily someone found me in time.

Several days later, my bed was visited by a strange woman. I was so surprised, I didn't let that in till you'd gone. You, of all people, come to visit me. It was difficult to appreciate, because good feelings come hard. Even after leaving hospital, I played games by coming round to Canterbury Crescent as an observer rather than because I knew I felt good about you (I've never risked my own insecurity, never dared to go more than a quarter of the way).

The myth was cracked when I started going with Sheila; she gave me a lot, but I didn't let any in really. I was too frightened to leave the pain of isolation. Isolation kept me secure in insecurity. I enjoyed the sarcasm from other people in Villa Road for joining 'Them'. Why was I joining 'the other side'? My body knew, but it wouldn't tell my head; that was too much, too soon. Now my head is coming back to join its body.

I still don't know about you though. Only the myths cultivated by people in Villa Road and an inkling of what you mean to people here at Atlantis. I want to find out for myself so . . . when are you coming back?

lots of love and warmth, Pete, x."

"Dear Magnificent Pete,

Hello, and I hope the sun is shining on your royal head. If the Oracle fulfills itself and you return here, then it is here we will join together to generate Madness, a commodity so sorely lacking in the utter drab sensibleness of Villa Road. If we are destined to meet on Inishfree, then rather I see myself resting my head on your lap in pain and crying out the sharp beauty of living and being alive and getting born and dying so often in one life-time. My real birth hasn't happened yet, but I feel it is not many months away. All my life up to now has been a nervous twitching, a restless kicking in the womb of fog that surrounds me and soon I sense the impending final crash as my head takes over in pure physicality and becomes merely a tool for pushing through into the real world. I don't know how heads got abstracted into the pretence that they are nothing to do with our bodies at all, or alternatively that they are all of us and our bodies don't exist. Well, you have a fine large head on you, Pete, and I will rub it for you, for there is a lot of pain there and even all that soft and fluffy hair cannot cushion you, because the pain throbs from inside and makes your eyes shrouded and your face so old, older than your years. I do believe you need to crawl down very small and allow your head to be taken over by a mother who this time will not be scared by you. For your own mother was so frightened of your head, she thought you were trying to kill her, she was terrified of you then and for the rest of your life and has tried to cover her fear in so many ways, ways she calls Love, but you must not believe her, because she would scream in terror if she really looked at you and knew that such a huge man had come out of her. She cannot face that terror, and so she cannot face you.

Pete, I will be here in London for considerably longer than expected; it is also possible that I shall be here for considerably shorter than expected, for it is an unfathomable mystery for us all to meditate upon that though the Future is undoubtedly Fixed, the present never is, it is eternally changing and unpredictable and alterable by our every action, it is a total learning experience and all pain comes of resisting the learning and fearing the next lesson and looking back in horror at past lessons, which if fully experienced would in fact contain no horror at all, for there would be no residue.

I love you and will see you soon, Jen."

Words from Anne to 'Peace News' on the occasion of them printing a hysterical article about Atlantis

"One-and-a-half years ago, I wrote to Jenny James telling her in a long and roundabout way that I desperately needed Primal Therapy immediately as I was cracking up and what could I do, please, please, as I had no money and could my friend Clare come with me and . . . She wrote back saying, 'Don't ask me to tell you what to do with your life. Come to Atlantis if you want to.'

Swallowing my indignation at getting such a snappy reply (what *had* I done to deserve it), me and my friend Clare packed our bags and set off for Atlantis.

Donegal never looked so bleak and black. Big black thunder clouds hung heavily in the sky. A storm was brewing. It was definitely an omen we thought as we walked shakily up the front path of this outrageously painted house. We got momentarily distracted by the bright colours and amazing astrological drawings from the dark doom that lay all around us, but we quickly pulled ourselves back together again to concentrate on the doom. We knew it was All Going to Happen on the other side of that brightly painted door.

'Oh, their potatoes are getting blighted,' I said, again distracted.

We knocked and entered. Two big black dogs loomed forward threatening, snarling, growling, eyeing my juicy flesh, but were pulled back by the warden, I mean woman, who owned them. She then introduced us to their twelve pups.

Clare and I stood in silence as we were allocated a room. 'Did we mind sharing as there were so many people in the house?'

'Why is everyone speaking so loud?' I wondered. It took me a long time to realize it's just that they weren't whispering, like I was used to doing.

That night, my friend and I lay in bed. The mattress was on the floor; we looked up at the ceiling about ten miles away. We dared not make a sound, as there was a big woman sleeping next door with her big guy. She had already told us to turn down a record player we had been playing. In the darkness and silence of the night, my friend and I whispered to each other. 'Clare, are you there?' I asked. 'Yes, Anne.' 'Clare, what are we doing here?' She didn't answer. We both lay frozen on the bed waiting at any moment for the entrance of twenty-eight vampires smiling saying, 'We've got you now. You can't get away from us.' The tension was too much and we both started giggling hysterically under the blankets, trying hard not to make a sound, which of course intensified our giggling. I felt like I was at church and trying not to laugh.

The next day, we had our first sessions. I said, 'After you, Clare.' She said, 'Oh, no, after you, Anne.' It was finally decided that she go first. I couldn't eat. I couldn't talk. I walked around. It was worse than any University exam or going out on stage. The moment came. I went into the Therapy Room. I lay down. 'Breathe', they said, 'and relax. Make a sound if you need to.' I then proceeded to make sounds. I screamed high. I screamed low. Short screams. Long screams. All making way and heading towards what I hoped would be the Primal Scream, that one Scream that began it all. Once I got back to that One Scream, I could start it all again. Ninety primal screams equals a cure, I thought. Surely at least ninety traumatic things happened to me as a child. Anyway, they let me scream and get a bit of a sore throat, but I felt great afterwards.

That night, I made dinner. I felt so tense at what people would say about my cooking that I ran out of the house and didn't come back until dinner was over.

Later on that night, I was in my first group. There were lots of different things going on between people to which I listened dutifully. Then, in the middle of it all, someone brought in tea. 'TEA?!! How can people drink tea at a moment like this?' I thought. 'What sacrilege!' Thoughts of food and drink were mere trivialities while all this grand feeling stuff was going on. How could they lower themselves? I held in my shocked feelings at this and at the girl beside me who was actually sewing.

After a while, it became obvious that I was going to be asked to say something, as nearly everyone in the room had spoken. I started to formulate sentences in my head. How could I sound spontaneous? How could I sound intelligent but feeling at the same time? How could I say the profoundest thing with the fewest words? Basically, how could I say 'the right thing'? My turn came. I spoke. I sounded quite normal. I laughed.

Was that me? 'Well, yes, actually it is rather nice to be here with all you people; I do feel a bit stiff though 'cause I haven't moved since I got into this room. Yes, it is rather exciting, but I feel a bit scared because I don't know what's going to come out of me. But yes, I do feel a new beginning; I do feel a gate has been opened and the sun is shining on a path that leads forward into the unknown, or rather the known but forgotten. I feel rather excited actually, and tingly. What amazing women there are here, so bright, energetic, and colourful. Gosh! – maybe it won't be all bad here after all!'

'Did you do those paintings on the walls, Jenny? They're really good.'

'Jill, will you teach me to ride the horse?'

'Graham, are you driving us to the beach now?'

'Felim, what are we going to do about the blighted potatoes?'

'Clare, do you know I haven't had a cigarette all day and I didn't even notice.'

'Becky, let's go and dance.'

It wasn't all sunshine and roses. Before I went to Atlantis, I was 'scared of angry women,' scared of jealous and vicious women. I discovered that I could be violent, angry, jealous and vicious. At the time, I would much rather have believed that I was gentle, kind and always loving, including when people were walking on me. But now I took a deeper breath and discovered a lioness who was just a bit pissed off with the meek and mild line, 'It's everyone else's fault and not mine'. Quite frankly, it was getting a bit boring living like that and no-one seemed to be interested anyway. I tried to convince everyone at first that I was weak, that I couldn't lead, I could only be led. People had always kicked me and put me down, how could anyone ask me to stand up? I wanted someone to beg me, to plead with me, to grovel in front of me, to be nice to me as I'd had it rough, to persuade me, to entice me, to give up their life for me. I felt pretty angry that no-one did this for me at Atlantis. Didn't everyone see that I'd had it the worst? I was a special case – I'd had it really bad. Tell me how nice I am, when I don't feel nice.

Tell me how important I am, when I don't feel important. Why don't you all love me, when I don't love myself? I can't help it if I feel hateful and jealous and murderous, love me anyway. I've got problems, can't you see?

People saw me all right. At first I didn't want to know what they saw. But then, remembering what my life had been like, I knew I didn't want to go backwards to that. So I trusted a little (what had I to lose?) and took a step forwards. I came out instead of going in. I waited for the blows to fall around my ears. None came. I waited for the put-down looks, the snide remarks, the comments that would shatter me to pieces inside. They never came.

In the beginning, I needed crutches to help me take the first few steps. Then I started walking on my own. Now I'm running, and soon I'll be ready to leap.

Anne."

AT ATLANTIS
How I get people into their feelings is
I offer to 'give' them Primal Therapy.

Up trots patient with briefcase full of expectations and books by Janov.
I carry on sweeping the kitchen floor.
Patient becomes impatient, and explodes or implodes.
I carry on sweeping the floor,
Learning to centre myself more,
In spite of people's explosions and implosions.
The floor gets swept.
The patient learns.

MONEY
People are taught to believe that money is real.
They can touch it, feel it, smell it, hear it.
It causes them Pain to make money;
So when they give money away,
They think they can give away their Pain

and purchase Pleasure.
Big mistake.
People give me their money,
and think I will buy their Pain.
But I say,
'Thank you very much for your money, I will spend it on land
and grass.
But you can keep your Pain.'
Some people leave disgusted because I refuse to buy their pain.
And they ask me for their money back.
I say, 'Your money is in the land and the grass. Please take all
you will.'
Then they get very angry indeed, because they do not want land
and grass.
What they want is a great big garbage dump for all their pain.

However,
When they get angry,
Miraculously, they lose their pain.
So I did take it away after all.
But Atlantis refuses to be a garbage dump
And insists on being
Quite simply beautiful.
Atlantis is the simplicity of each person
Before they turned into garbage dumps.
We say: Please dump your garbage back where it belongs
And come and enjoy the land and the grass.

Lots of people want to destroy Atlantis;
They hate us because we show them their soul.
Having your soul bared can be painful,
Especially when you think it is Black.
Out there, no-one ever again shows them their soul;
And so they think they have lost it
And that we have stolen it away;
Because they knew they had a soul when they were at Atlantis.

There is another way of leaving Atlantis,
And that is by taking Atlantis with you.
People who take Atlantis away with them,
And live in it,
Never feel like destroying anything.

You don't feel your chains till you start to move.
So no-one wants to move: chains hurt.
So everyone keeps very still.
And the more you don't move, the rustier your chains get
And the less you feel like moving.
Eventually, your chains drag you down to death.
It's no good waiting for a biological incentive to move.
It won't come.
Your only impulse will be to keep very still.
Your only hope is your brain.
You have to use your head to break the spells that bind.
Use your head to move your arse, to feel your chains and yell
your pain.
Once you move, you'll feel your chains as weights to be
shaken off.
And shaking becomes a joy.
Some of you won't hear me, won't ever know it's true.
Some of you will hear me, but won't know what to do.
Some of you will do it, and then you'll always know
YOU DON'T FEEL YOUR CHAINS TILL YOU START TO
MOVE.

We are a primal commune.
We don't accept anything secondary.
We focus on what is of prime importance.
When civilization crumbles and the illusion of shops and the
safety of concrete and the cover of clothes is lost, we have
nothing but our mouths, our fingers and our eyes. We have one
another, and the sky and the sea.
At Atlantis, we destroy illusions.

People who have their ego invested in their illusions do not
like us.
They feel we are destroying them.
People coming to Atlantis should not read the Primal Scream.
They should read the I Ching.

If you fancy yourself
As an ant or a bee,
Then stay in London, stay at school and go to University.
They will teach you how to receive and obey orders
And how to live in a perfectly ordered society with so much to do
that you can keep your mind off the fact
that your centre is outside of yourself
and you are living and working for Someone Else

Me, I fancy myself as a she-goat,
wild and free, calm and skippy, playful and mischievous
damnably annoying if you try to catch her and pin her down.
Pushy, loving and appreciative
Sexy, lazy, motherly and proud.
Goats are simple, and never ever boring.
Ants and bees are complicated. And predictable.
They're good at maths and engineering.
Me, I just know how to give milk,
And eat grass.

1978

ATLANTIS YEAR FOUR: WINTER

Winter is the most exciting season of the year.

Winter is when all that has been sinks down into the ground to make it rich and ready for a regeneration of life. Winter is when we clear away last year's remains and dig the earth thoroughly, turning it over ready for spring planting. Winter is when we bring home all our animals and keep them near us around the house and garden. Winter is a time for consolidation, for looking back at what has been and looking forward to what is coming and working very hard with what is.

I am writing this review of Atlantis 1978 as Winter 1979 approaches. I have just spent two days reading over six thick letter-files for 1978. The energy in them is phenomenal, each happening would make a story in itself. And that is just what is going to happen: Atlantis 1978 and 1979 will form the basis of a new book. So, here, only a taste of these two past years will be given.

Basically, Atlantis 1978 was the year of the Grand Clearout, when we finally and absolutely gave up the concept of this being primarily a 'therapy commune.' That image had brought us more problems than people: we were seen as a garbage tip for everyman's neurosis. Oh goody goody a place to go and flop and groan and moan. So our motto changed from die first, live later to an insistence that people came here first and foremost to LIVE. The result was that there was more 'therapy' than ever before, intenser, realer, organically, intricately linked with our everyday living and loving and working and hating. Compared with other growth centres, Atlantis had always been like that, but now Selfishness became an absolute rule. We were no longer willing to sell ourselves and our time for money. People still came, and they brought their skills and their money, and we guaranteed absolutely nothing in return, except that they'd be joining one of the most fantastic alive communities in Europe: anything they got, they'd have to *take,* there'd be no more dutiful giving or buying of 'help' in the Realm of Atlantis. One of the many results of this was an even greater intensification of passions raging about us: people adored us more, and hated us to death.

The gap between Atlantis and the Rest of the World was widening; it was terrifying, it was exciting, and we loved it. We loved ourselves more as others loved us less. Our language and our concepts became more and more tribal, our attitudes more extremely different from the 'ruling ideology' outside. What we were experiencing was what would happen if any group of people got cut off on a desert island from the mainstream of cultural merging, and formed their own ways, lived from their own instincts and needs. We got hotter, more colourful, more beautiful, more creative. We entirely gave up trying to please, and we pleased ourselves more.

1978 began with the delivery of the nicest Christmas present anyone could ever receive: my sister Snowy. I had been estranged from her for four years. She 'phoned me up just before the Christmas holiday and said, Could she come to Atlantis for a week? Surprised, reserved, but friendly, I said, 'Certainly.' I felt she was very brave; we had never got on, and I didn't expect it to be any different once the initial rush of energy at the reunion was past.

She never left. Her week extended to a life-time. Snowy is now a Queen of Atlantis in her own right, one of our greatest assets. Two years younger than myself, she was still nearly a decade older than most of the young women here, and she brought with her years of experience, struggle and leadership in her own urban scene in Lancaster, England; years of experience in running therapeutic groups, participating in communal living situations and helping to organize all kinds of community-based social projects. Her life and mine had since our early years moved in opposite directions, so it seemed: she towards fairly conventional involvement, myself always further out on to a strange revolutionary limb. Now the natural curve of our life paths brought us full circle, and we met.

Snowy came to Atlantis, saw what she needed, packed up everything, sold her house in Lancaster, and invited her friends – all 129 of them – to join her. Each one refused. So she broke with all of them, kidnapped her two children from their respective fathers and joined the black sheep of Atlantis. Her name and ours are now passwords to awe and gossip and horror stories all over Lancaster. Snowy Flames, as we call her, merely grins and flows and grows. One thing about moving onwards at your own rate is there are no regrets and no-one can jump on your back because you don't keep still long enough.

The first month or so at Atlantis, my sister spent letting herself be really ill, letting out all the tension and confusion of her past relationships. We all worked with her, giving her dozens of sessions. Sometimes she went a bit far, even for us, especially when she threatened to bleed to death each time she had a period. Once we had to take her to hospital for a blood transfusion, but when they threatened her with an operation, she put her foot down, stopped bleeding immediately and therapy did the rest.

As the months passed by, Snowy's leadership qualities began to flower; she took over the island gardens; she began to write; and then, blissfully, she finally began to organize me, a luxury I rarely enjoyed in my life. My sweetest memory is of September 1978 when Snowy put a notice on the kitchen door saying: 'Jenny James does not exist. All 'phone calls, enquiries and requests to Snowy.' I wrote at the time:

28th September, 1978
"Days and days of the most intense beauty and learning and strength and despair and pain. A communal last-ditch stand to save our lives. Snowy takes over and the sky heaves a sigh of relief. 'At last they are understanding,' say the gods. The little sister has to take her place at the head of the household; she finds her ways and her methods and her stern Taurean strength. She sees. All snakes who do not understand the principle of living for oneself and not by vamping on others must scuttle off. The wheels whirr rapidly. An RTE camera crew bring yet another Atlantean era to a magnificent, bloody and colourful close. Jim is there on film; a pale and bewildered Dubliner.

I don't think he ever has the time to stand and see; the hurdy-gurdy merry-go-round horror house is too fast moving. But he has the trust of a child on a big dipper. I never had that kind of trust: I had to learn it. I love the people I hate when I am resting! Damien, another Dubliner, has his trust too. It is not every bent and awkward Irishman who subjects himself to the majesty and terror of this mediaeval establishment where mediocrity is not tolerated and the children run wild. And Alu, our dozy German, who tells the cameramen, 'I came here for an accident.' He got his accident all right. All the brave and scared people, hundreds of them, coming and going and returning and going, life-blood of Atlantis.

Snowy's greatest bravery is to dare to be authoritarian in the face of the crushing threat of universally accepted oppressive depressive compulsory Liberalism, the greatest mindfuck and bullshit of all time. Dear goats, please be kind, think of me and do not butt me; Cow, would you mind please containing your shitting till you leave the barn; and you, Stallion, kindly train yourself to withhold your erection in company.

It was at this time that my sister and Chris encouraged me gently but firmly to cut off all my long dark scruffy hair. All of it. Right down to the last half inch. I have had long hair all my life. I am hung-up about my face. I like to hide it. 'More, Jen, all those fluffy bits; let's see your ears.' I cut and cut, trusting them. I bared my face completely; I cropped my hair close to my head. We look at me, to see what four Atlantean years, 36 Earth years and a hundred different relationships had made of me on my chosen life-path. I am pale; they said I looked awfully tired. I felt myself as a celibate priestess, slim and clean and alone: delicate. I dressed myself in brown and white shapeless robes and felt exposed to the atmosphere. Now the sun could shine on me, the wind had nothing to blow, the rain wet all of my face. I was never a pretty girl, but I felt soft and beautiful within myself.

Jim confirms all my previous fears; he hates what I have done to my hair; he says I look hard and ugly and dreadful.

I look him in the eyes and I do not flinch and his face is far from hard or ugly as he tells me; it is soft and beautiful and smiling. He talks on, talks himself through his initial stage of images until he is saying I look vulnerable and easy to hurt; and he is crying.

I lie in bed today, an aching head and body. I have so much to learn about how to take without hurting myself. Jim, a child from another universe. The new demoted Jenny, who is she without her responsibilities? A child who never had time. I race, I run; my sister slows me down, conquers me where no man bothers. She is the most beautiful and extreme person I ever met. I am the most fragile and difficult person she ever met.

I am tired. So many times I thought I would die. I stopped saving other people's lives. I decided to save my own. As the great Snowy says: 'Everything is perfect. If you feel bad, it is because you are in some way resisting the perfection of the moment you are in.'

Yes, 1978, clearing time. We cleared our house completely. We changed the rooms, and the people. We set up a beautiful craft shop in the front room where the therapy room used to be. We threw our house open to the public, we became more public even than we used to be. We changed the kitchens, knocked down walls, altered everything. I painted more murals, covered the whole house from top to bottom, in and out, with more colour. Through not advertising any more to 'give therapy', as predicted, we found a new sort of person turning up. People who walked on their own two feet; people who wanted to give and share instead of just take; people interested in living, in living communally, in building, in learning.

And then we all turned psychic. Just like that. I'd been using my psychic powers unbeknown to myself for years in helping people in therapy. And I'd always known there was something 'special' about my Scorpio daughter. Now our powers really flowed. We sat in awe listening to Becky. Then one day I discovered by accident that I had photographically accurate clairvoyant insight. So of course my sister tried; she was the most brilliant of all. Later, we passed it on; Chris could do it of course; and so could Liam, and Sean and Les – anyone in fact, who is willing to let the cosmos flow in and out of them without restriction. We started peeping into other worlds. We got excited. We started peeping beyond death. Reincarnation stared us slap bang in the face. We stared at one another. Excuse me, isn't this supposed to be a sensible down-to-earth, materialistic kind of commune? Well, I don't know about the sensible. We closed our doors more and more, turned in to enjoy our new discoveries, delved and dug and dipped in, learnt how to tune in to anyone, anywhere, to know their thoughts and feelings. Black magic? Oh yes, there's always a Bad Name for anything enjoyable, for anything that is powerful and colourful and that changes the world.

1978, year too of the 'Atlantis Road Show', Atlantis taken out to the streets, mostly by my sister: our dressing-up and our fun and dance and antics and cheek and tricks and philosophies bundling noisily and relievingly through the greyness of strife-torn Belfast; causing trouble in violence-ridden London; erupting in liberal Lancaster; our theories and our practice, our anti-society-as-it-is awfulness, our utter refusal to lie down under any social pressure or behaviour laws, taken right out into the Great Outside. Atlantis turned up on a ship at Larne: what is this? A band of flamboyant, seductive Atlanteans breeze past the reluctant, protesting boat-guardians to give a flashy, rowdy send-off to some white-faced tight-lipped men who had come to have a bad time at Atlantis and left in a huff when they found they couldn't. These crazy Atlanteans travel 150 miles just to show them Life Rules OK? 'Atlancaster' sets up in Snowy's old street so she can feel the weight of years of having to play it cool, tame herself down, keep herself under and within limits; Snowy took it to the limit in her old town and then leapt beyond. She lost as many friends in five minutes as I have boasted of losing in five years. Atlantis goes to London, the most dangerous and sophisticated city of all, where 'left-wing' squatters knife you and organize gangs if you show too much liveliness; where it is the height of revolutionariness to live in drabness, dark and dirt; where to clean and clear up, to sing and shout and cry and have things out with one another; to be against drugs and dossing around is 'fascistic.' Oh yes, Atlantean ways were well-tested on the streets and in the pubs and city dwellings in 1978.

WINTER means coming into full maturity; a purring readiness for new growth, new paths, new heights. A tremendous excitement: what next? The winds blow fast and fresh in winter; the earth is deeply pondering, digesting all that has gone before, concocting new spells for the coming year.

Atlantis 1978 saw a new speed, a new gear. Previously, people had stayed at Atlantis up to three years, 'going through their growth.' And still it was complained that Atlantis was too fast, too pushy, too extreme, too intolerant. In 1978, we got worse! We tightened our boundaries, upped our demands, on one another, on ourselves, on life. Entry into Atlantis was as easy as ever: the door is open and you walk in. But after that, the poor newcomer was left dangling in mid-space. No more the comfy 'therapy' label. No more the neat 'sessions' (not that our sessions were ever very neat). No. What Atlantis offered was a working example of how to live, a method daily displayed of how to sort out every possible hurdle in the way of living. Those that were ready to be inspired, jumped in breathless, nervous and excited. Those who felt they needed more structured pathways left, grumbling. We upped our standards for ourselves, and the result was more people, more flow, more energy, more gifts and excitement, more trouble, an even eviler reputation, and an even better life.

★   ★   ★

Here is Colm's story:
"The first time I heard of Atlantis, I was hitching from Bunbeg to Dungloe. I was so terrified I didn't even dare go into Burtonport to look at this strangely painted house, and all I knew about the place was that *it* was a commune and *they* were mostly English and sounded very lively and noisy people – hence

the name 'Screamers'. Just the thought of so much fun, life and colour kept me well clear. After all, I had just spent two months on a farm in Sligo and I thought that if only I could get myself a farm, work hard with cows and sheep, then most of my worries would be solved. Solidness and contentment was what I wanted. Anybody too lively was disturbing and best left alone – though somewhere in me, I was moved by the vivid image I found in my head when told about the Screamers. I was definitely *not* going to get myself involved.

Two-and-a-half years later, I came again to Donegal, again to buy a farm, and this time, although apprehensive, I was aware enough now to know that even though I told myself I had come to Ireland to live on a farm alone, somewhere up on a hillside, really what I wanted was to live with other people and enjoy the life and energy of a commune. And Atlantis sounded the right place. There was therapy there and a commune with therapy was bound to work. So, after two months of indecision, an Atlantis search party found me and invited me back. My first contact with the shining giants of Atlantis had left me still intact – Jenny James and her acolytes were to all intents and purposes human and lots of fun.

Imagine a household where the adults behave like children rushing around dressing up, laughing, men and women crying and fighting. Imagine grown-ups teasing each other: just like when I was first at school – terrifying games I daren't join in but which made me laugh all the time from the sheer fun and excitement. A whole kitchen-load of people turning on a fully grown man and forcing him to answer questions he obviously didn't want to answer and all of us just laughing when he came across confused and stupid. I remember gangs at school, the power and energy in joining, but also the horror and fear if maybe that gang would turn against me. At school, there were no limits, and sometimes playtime was too long and all I wished for was the safety of the classroom and the controlling atmosphere of 'authority' and schoolwork. Anything was better than the mad Anarchy of a kids' playground. Imagine fully mature women, instead of acting the calm schoolteachers, letting themselves loose on the playground!

What I thought I had left behind in my childhood found me again for better and for worse. Except this time there was no welcome break for lessons, no home except Atlantis. These Atlanteans wanted total involvement, sleeping, eating and playing together.

In spite of my serious cover, I have always been easily affected by fun and excitement. I am easily distracted from the 'homely' pretence I try and keep up. In fact, the truth is that self-sufficiency, jam-making and digging the garden were only a refuge from the total confusion I would get into whenever I joined with any lively energetic group of people, and, thinking back, I always did seem to find such people wherever I went. Inevitably, as I settled some place, I would sooner or later seek out those who would unsettle me.

And so I found Atlantis. Without a murmur of regret, I wheeled my 28in. wheel policeman's bicycle into the barn, changed my clothes and joined up with the living, letting myself take shape and colour amongst new friends. I was now living riotously with people who actually thrived on change and movement and who accepted nothing but the truth whether simple or horrendous – only the truth made any impression on them. This was a shaky business! After all, I had spent most of my life running away from myself and here I was, bubbling over with energy, having the best time of my life and also, horror of horrors, finding it increasingly impossible to stop all the madness and nastiness coming up from where I normally kept them.

All right, Atlantis was the place to let these dark secrets out, but I didn't want to destroy my friendships so soon; better to play cool for a while and not let myself go with all this excitement. Nastiness? Madness? What do you mean?

Just imagine someone from whom you can get what you need in life: love, warmth and friendship. And then suddenly, you find yourself annoyed by them; but help! not just irritated, but angry with the same passion and energy you have been living

with for the last week, and what's worse, you can't feel the end
of this anger dredged up from places you've never before allowed
the light of living to enter. You imagine total destruction of
your friend, of the room, murder and carnage all around, and
only a small chance of yourself surviving the holocaust. Considering your friend had only momentarily reminded you of
your mother, or just mentioned how much a previous lover had
meant to her, and considering your friend's unaggressive manner,
you believe yourself to be suffering from over-excited halluci-
nations or whatever your personal vice might be, and you
quickly put away such craziness and try to go even more energetically forward to brighter and better things.

Unfortunately, holding back that much anger requires an
equal amount of life energy, so after a few more internal
implosions, containment is a definite problem. Leakages might
occur. You hope you are the only one who knows what is going
on inside you. Everyone else continues living their fantastically
full lives all over the place. You feel terrible physically and
mentally. You know asking for help will eventually uncover the
volcano, so you settle for a reduced standard of living, hope
no-one notices, and that the wind will change.

They do, and it doesn't. Everybody does notice the state
you're in, and things get even worse.

If at this stage you truly do want contact and friendship and
you express this need, you at least reopen channels to other
humans and you have a chance to stand among the living again,
for the one outstanding beauty of Atlantis is that friendship and
love are always easy to find if asked for.

More likely, however, your present resentment at not being
able to join in the fun (not surprising considering what you're
having to hold back), provides a perfect outlet for all your pent-
up rage: silently, in your head, you begin torturing one by one
the inhabitants of Atlantis.

Only one problem: the inhabitants of Atlantis somehow know
what you're doing. They say they can *feel* the pains in their
bodies and would you stop please. Well, actually, as attack is

the best means of defence, you're usually confronted by anything from one person to the entire household who seem to be keeping themselves alive and entertained at your expense. Songs and jokes are made up about you. There is no limit to what these elusive magicians can do. By now, your entire life force – what's left over, that is, after you've held back that enormous ball of fire that's stampeding round your body, is centred around methods of Revenge and Escape. *They* definitely would like you back amongst the living, so that is certainly *not* what you're going to do and if only your mind wasn't so preoccupied with hate, you could think up a way to get away without them seeing you.

There are solutions preferred by Atlanteans which would enable you to stay within the limits of their kingdom: live on the island, go to their house in London. But what fun you have in refusing co-operation. Dismissal of friendship is revenge which doesn't require any energy. Cutting off protects your dark secrets all the more.

At some low level, you are still human and should some basic instinct be touched in you, you can still react: someone's intense pain; the need to survive, to defend yourself from attack, would cause you to move yourself. But as soon as you mobilize yourself, guess what else awakens: that evil darkness, destruction, lightning, fire and flames. All are there waiting and you are now truly frightened. No way will you look at such chaos and carnage. Now is the time to go. Now before you feel that evil stirring inside you again. Now quick, speed and flash. Fear helps you and you manage to get out, to escape to the outside world, a world of calmness which soothes your jumbled fear. Fear leads you, acts for you, you go far away from That Place where you sensed the Beast you carry in you, for that beast you are sure came from the House and belongs there. The fear is only there when you think of Atlanteans and for months you know it's still there ready to rise and send you running.

But living in the outside world brings its own troubles. Frustration; the non-fulfilment of being half-dead most days

and always having Atlantis to measure your life by. Fear of
not being able to be alive again except through alcohol or drugs;
and you're getting older. Fear of being alone because relating
to other people is hard. Your standards are higher these days
and you demand more of your partners. So in the end, as you
fight to live, you think more and more of Atlantis House, where
in spite of all the terror, you remember living once in a fairyland
of magic with Kings and Queens as your friends.

And so one day, you find yourself standing in front of the
door, bringing yourself back to live once again amongst the
Golden People from Atlantis.

There was snow on the ground as I waited for my lift from
Fintown to Burtonport and more snow falling softly. I felt at
ease. I was going back, back to where I could learn to fly again.
After five months away, I wanted to go back. I knew Atlantis
was where I should be and I seemed to know I would be welcome. A sureness because just me coming back showed how
much the magic had entered into me. I was sure that was all
I needed do: tell everyone how I had never stopped thinking
about them in five months, and how when I stopped running and
looked around me, the only place I could see with life was the
palace of Atlantis.

My return was a song in itself as it told how living really is
worthwhile, worth all the fear. This is what kept me going till
I reached that door. I walked into the house in tears seeking
only one thing. From behind a closed door, women's laughter.
And before I knew, I was inside the room amidst the laughing
faces of these people who stand so big they fill the room and
who give every human act the energy and colour of a lifetime.
Jenny, who had been my lover, Empress and Ruler, and who
had forced me to look at my own hidden violence. I could hold
her now and feel excitement and pleasure. Snowy, her sister,
full of strength and the passion of being a woman. And visiting
princes whom I knew only by sight. Somewhere, too, would be
Becky, first-born of Atlantis; and Christine, her sister-in-fun.

The house felt full of bodies. I had come back to where humans lived and showed their living.

I was so excited by the contact with life again, that I didn't eat for two days, my energy was buzzing too fast for such mundane needs as food. And I didn't feel the cold either. In the middle of winter, I wore fewer clothes than most people wear in summer. I kept me alive with love and energy. (So much for the hallucinated world-wide energy crisis!)

While I had been gone, Jenny had been in a deep personal struggle to keep alive in a relationship which had awakened her own death layers. So I came home to find her pale, and I felt like a healer, a juggler flowing coloured globes of light through my hands. The colours and movements of life, the complexities and excitements of living – my show was involving my whole life force; my body danced with my hands to guide me. I am the Lord of Light, of the dancing lights. No-one can resist me, for my magic is for amusement with no purpose save demonstration of what is already there.

Jenny responded slowly; her damage is strong. But she looked up and walked forward to clearer air."

Colm Thompson

★ ★ ★

Annoyingly enough for those who would denigrate our seemingly crazy, chaotic, unbridled life-style, the external result of such living is clear-headed, fluently-spoken, straight-spined, dignified but sparkling adults who can hold their own in any situation whatever. Faced with reporters, with audiences of social workers, with visiting priests and nuns, with a week-long intensive of RTE cameras, with police or health officials, our case comes across calmly, convincingly and so obviously backed-up by the light in our eyes, the fluency of our thought and movement, and the roses in our cheeks, not to mention our ease with one another: our ability to reprimand, banter, disagree, touch, encourage, interrupt, bow down to one another, as occasion demands. Consequently, as our reputation got worse and worse with those who never met us, but only heard about us – like the 'alternative' and 'progressive' and 'leftwing' elements in England and Ireland, our actual contacts, which included local people and officials of all kinds, got better and better. Many years ago, a clairvoyant told me that 'Atlantis would become more and more rooted in the community and take on a more 'conventional' image.' I was vaguely indignant, but quite amused, sensing instinctively what this could mean, but never visualizing it as it actually came about:

'SUNDAY INDEPENDENT', Sunday, September 10th, 1978
HEALTH BOARD REFERS BOY TO 'SCREAMERS'
Exclusive by Trevor Danker

A 19-year-old Donegal youth has been referred by social workers to stay with members of the commune in Burtonport, Co. Donegal, known locally as 'The Screamers'.

The North-Western Health Board confirmed that they had referred other people they had been dealing with to the commune . . .

Bernard Cawley, who has no parents, has spent most of his life in hospitals and foster homes.

He was given the option by social workers, who have been looking after his welfare, of living in the Rehabilitation Hostel in Dublin, sharing a flat or trying life in the commune.

He chose Atlantis House, although he didn't realize who was living there until he arrived at the front door of the gaily-coloured house.

When I spoke to Bernard, a frail, bespectacled youth, on Wednesday – less than 24 hours after he got there – he was absolutely thrilled with the idea of living there.

'I had seen them on television, but I did not realize I was going to stay with them until I saw the paintings on the walls of the house.

'When we drove up, I thought: 'They have sent me to a load of nuts'. But it's not like that at all. They are all very nice.'

Meanwhile, the two social workers, Olga Garland and Michelle Hart, who suggested Atlantis House as an option for Bernard, defended the choice when I spoke to them.

Miss Garland of the North-Western Health Board told me, 'Our only concern is for Bernard's welfare. He has had a very difficult life and we wanted to find somewhere he wanted to go and where he would be happy.

'We gave him the choice of three places to go because we didn't want to force him to go anywhere he wasn't happy with. He chose Atlantis House.

'The North-Western Health Board have not come down in favour or against the commune there. I think people should know what they are doing before wildly condemning them.

'I have been round their house and seen how they live twice – once with Kevin Murphy, who was at the time our Director of Community Care.

'I have also met and talked to Jenny James, the girl who founded the commune three or four years ago, several times. I was one of about fifty social workers from the North West who attended a lecture Jenny gave some time ago.

'We have to decide every case we handle on its individual merit. I felt it would not be wrong in Bernard's circumstances to suggest that he might like to live there. But there was no question of forcing him to go there or that he did not know where he was going.

I have suggested Atlantis House to other people we have been dealing with. But only as an option if they wanted to go there themselves.'

Jenny James, the English girl who founded the commune just over three years ago, told me she had been contacted a few times by social workers to see if they had room for people they wanted to refer to them.

'We have always taken them willingly, but none of them have ever stayed for any length of time. I think that Bernard might, though.' . . .

When I left Bernard, he was drinking tea and chatting happily to two or three other members of the commune.

It could be an inspired choice after all.

1979

ATLANTIS YEAR FIVE: SPRING

JJ in London, February 1979

Central heating in my brain
My creativity down the drain.
Give me the breezes of Inishfree
Life I can feel, death I can see.

This is the cry of a creature in London
Left the green fields to find people, but found none;
Everyone locked in their own personal mess;
Won't you just stop a moment while I give my address?

I've a lovely big house and an island in Eire
Search though you may, I doubt you'll find fairer;
We're a bunch of good women, as fine as you've dreamed of
We're soft and we're gentle, though our name may be
     screamed of.

Atlantis our house, Atlantis our home,
Inishfree our island, we love every stone.
We till it and tend it and invite you to share
The work and the love and to lay yourself bare . . .

To the eyes and the hearts of women whose core
Is deeply explored, and covered no more
With tricks and deceptions and old games galore.
No, we'll open our arms if you also are raw.

But for any who come and try to pretend,
With wide open mouths, but eyes that defend,
We have sensitive antennae that endlessly extend
Into any dark corner, round each foul-smelling bend.

Witches we are, and black ones we'll be
To any who say that all they can see
Is a garden of roses when inside their head
Is a pit full of snakes all trying to play dead.

Our culture is different, for inside our tribe
Clean violence we welcome, false sweetness can't bribe.
We know that each human is both devil and god
So don't wave your gold wand if it's a threatening rod.

If it's roughness you feel, we won't put you down;
If it's sadness that chokes you, then cry till you drown.
But don't try to be nice if your instincts say, 'Kill!'
At Atlantis, the reward for politeness is nil.

★ ★ ★

'DONEGAL PEOPLE'S PRESS', 9th February, 1979
HOAX PARCEL BOMB SENT TO 'SCREAMERS'

Army personnel were called to 'The Screamers' Commune, Burtonport, on Wednesday evening, to deal with a suspected parcel bomb.

The alert was raised when the parcel, which had a postmark in the Republic, was delivered to the Commune. Preliminary investigation showed that it contained batteries and wires.

The house was immediately cleared of its eight occupants and the house sealed off by the Gardai.

Following the arrival of army bomb experts, the package was destroyed by a controlled explosion. It was found that it did not contain any explosives.

★ ★ ★

In 1979, Atlantis began all over again. What a strange year! The five-month long postal strike and our increasingly radical attitudes, our increasingly high demands on ourselves and those living with us, our new policy of not sitting around waiting for people to 'go dead' on us, but of firmly putting them on the doorstep, sometimes meant that Atlantis consisted of myself, my sister and my daughter Rebecca, now a fully blossomed, magnificently powerful 16-year-old witch. Those were indeed times of soul-searching as we weeded the beans!

"Er, Jenny,' my sister would say, "You don't think we're being just a bit too radical, do you? I mean, I'm leaving for Scotland soon, Becky's away in London, there's just that one girl looking after the island, and you're here writing a book about a *commune.*'

Times of heart-searching, times of torment, times of hilarity and high spirits, hysterical times when we discovered our big house could ring with the noise and laughter of – just the two of us, sisters who all our childhood had been firm enemies. Times of writing and creativity; a time for me to break through my singing and music-playing blocks; a time for my sister to face a thousand horror-trips inside herself about me, her big sister. A time for Becky to go over and over her painful feelings about her long-lost father, to spend the whole year in fact preparing herself for her long-term autumn departure into the Grand Outside.

A time of surprises, of returnings of Old Leavers; of thank-you letters from those who had left as enemies; a time for re-establishment of contact all around. A time when so many people called the local police on us, that the local police got to know us really well and to like us so much that each new visit from them was accompanied by a sigh, a wink and a grin. A time for reversal of our own English leftwing anti-police prejudices! and for recognition of the utter differentness of Irish rural society from anything any of us had ever known: rural Ireland, where everything is ruled by personal contact, by emotional pulls and swings, by moods of the moment, by vendetta and forgiveness, by punches and handshakes. Ireland, the natural organic home of 'that weird place they call the Screamers.'

Snowy, walking down the street one day, was stopped by a local man. 'It's not true you're selling the house, is it?' he said, quite upset. 'Yes,' said Snowy, 'but only to move to the island.' 'Oh, thank goodness,' he said, 'I'd hate to see you leave.' As far as we knew, the only contact that old fellow had had with us was buying our calf.

1979, the year when I managed to strand myself for two days and nights in the middle of March on a small, bare, windswept, rain-drenched island to try and make friends with a load of my billy-goats who had gone wild on me. The billies got quite used to me, but I couldn't get used to myself, and the horror and destruction inside of me. Living in a barely body-sized cave, I went through a kind of post-nuclear-war nightmare inside myself; nowhere inside me could I find any colour or life or safety or warmth. In what we later came to call the 'Inismil Experience' (the name of the island), I had to feel my own utter desolation, the wreckage of this century we live in manifest in my own body and mind, my own total need for my friends to keep me alive and rooted with some pleasure in this world. I could not recommend the experience to anyone, and yet we all have to go through it, for I am sure it is our universal truth: too many others have given me reflections of the same phenomenon for it to be coincidence. It is the price we have paid for cutting ourselves off from the fountains of real life, from the earth and animals and growth around us, from each other and from our own instincts. After ten years of intense full-time non-stop dedicated passionate working on myself in the most radical therapy available, this was still my inner reality. And it can't be changed, it can only be felt, worked with, accepted as one's core of truth from which to relate to the people we need. In 1969, I went into a therapy I hoped would 'rid me of my need for other people.' In 1979, my independence and strength is based on my complete surrender to that need.

★   ★   ★

I have just spent two days going through the horrors about this book. Now I am back at my typewriter again. 23rd September, 1979. Thirty-five hens running miserable in the rain outside my evening window, waiting to be fed.

I love September; autumn makes me want to cry. The summer at Atlantis is too full: one long hubbub of visitors, hitch-hikers, bed-and-breakfasters, brief stayers, millions of Germans, WWOOFERs (an English organization, 'Weekend Workers on Organic Farms'). Last weekend we had a big anti-Uranium mining Festival at Atlantis with street theatre, puppet shows,

live music, dancing, masses of vegetarian food, dozens of posters
and banners, film and video-shows, leafletting and public speaking. Now we are settling in for the winter. Jam-making in the
kitchen. Egg-preserving; peat fires again; the potatoes being dug
and laid up in the attics; beautiful potatoes this year, the blight
passed us by in spite of us not using any chemicals. The goats
have to be mated again soon. I'm glad we sold the cows; unhappy creatures.

Colm is back yet again. An Atlantean recidivist, one of many.
Ned is back too, another trier. It is always a good feeling when
someone returns to Atlantis for another try, another attempt to
face the unfaceable, to breathe into the unbearable, to stand up
and be counted.

I am the commune ogre. I am everybody's projection screen.
I am also Jenny, very lost lately. I am having to face my need
to be injected with another's energy in order to feel rooted in
this world. I am not being supplied with my daily injection,
and so I flounder and lose touch and feel hopeless and think
Atlantis is made of mud and what the hell am I doing writing
a book to 'help' other people, and what *is* this weird place called
Atlantis anyway? Yes, I too lose the magic, regularly. And when
I lose it, I cannot believe that anything bright ever happened.
I read back over past correspondence and feel only sick; I suspect my highs, start to think all my good feelings were phoney,
that all my good perceptions of people, and all my angers, were
nothing but projections of my own insides, and that I wasn't
seeing the people I was relating to at all.

But then I did a psychic reading: this is one of the many ways
we have at Atlantis of understanding each other, feeling one
another from inside, looking for a while through another person's eyes. In this way, we also separate ourselves from each
other, we know what is you and what is me, when things are
becoming muggy and unclear. We discover our amazing
similarities, and our amazing differences. And we shift both our
own energy, and the other person's, and feelings flow again.

And so now I feel I can talk again, to people I will never meet. Now I feel once more that I have something to say, not just a hysterical outpouring, but the essence of the sound, earthbound magic that is Atlantis: which is to go into hell pits, grovel in them, choke nearly to death, and rise up crying or smiling and flow once more inside ourselves and with one another, with people we never wanted to breathe the same air as again. It happens in everyone's life of course; nothing can happen here that doesn't happen everywhere. Each one of us knows the ecstasy of flow and the horrors of stagnation and death between people. Atlantean magic lies in the speed-up, the activation and taking charge of the process. I, who have invented a million clever, funny and artistic ways for people to come alive, reach rock bottom regularly, where nothing flows and all creativity goes. Flat, dull, boundaryless, energyless, hopeless, meaningless, pointless. But I have a perfect slave-driver who will not let me rest, except constructively – sinking into my morass and feeling what it is like down there, so that I will come up shining, wiping the mud from my limbs and producing miracles once more. My slave-driver is myself, is Atlantis, is this magical and horrifying station I have set up out of my own need, with the rigid rules and morals and ethics, with the messianic purpose; the place no-one can bear, least of all myself. Atlantis, place of no illusion, of no hidey-holes. Here we have to look at the twentieth century and all it entails. It is not a pretty picture. But the deeper you delve, the higher you can fly; no magic can come out of mediocrity; but if you grapple with the essence of Mordor, the reward is life in Lothlorien.

Just two weeks ago, when I heard of doings of Colm in Galway, when he was cut off from us once more, I despised him, I looked down on him, I had nothing but contempt for him; I saw him as an empty opportunist flitting aimlessly round the world. I never wanted him back here; and I never thought I would see him again, not for a long time anyway. Then he walked back in again, as so often before, and I was rigid against him; though I did admit behind his back that Atlantis always flowers and flows the more fluidly for his presence. And it is true. Each person who comes to stay here and who takes charge of themselves, alters the face of Atlantis. Colm has his own special ways. He brings the zittery magic of fear and insecurity, of movement and colour, of technical skills and homely kitchen skills, of excitement about the future. He brings his total acceptance of all the childish practical madness which is Atlantis, our crazy plans for when the End of the World comes, when we will build a twentieth century Ark and sail away just in time to meet the rising of the old Atlantis as Europe and America sink beneath the nuclear waves. Colm and I are in tune. Colm and Atlantis are in tune. Because Colm is in tune with himself. He is the Magician in the Tarot. Everyone has magic, and Atlantis is the place to bring it out. Where else is magic appreciated? Daily, over breakfast? I have not found anywhere else. Loving Atlantis means loving life. We atheists are religious about our love for life. We have a saying, 'If you really live in Atlantis, you take it with you wherever you go.' My sister and daughter are at present away from Atlantis; but I know that whatever is happening around them is magic; they have the spell upon them, the special Atlantean shine to their faces which everyone sees and either hates or falls passionately in love with. It is the sparkle of craziness that has no twists, a craziness that is perfectly coherent and energetic and does not lurk in dark corners. It is the craziness of being so alive and vulnerable, that the hand of the killer is stayed in awe.

★ ★ ★

The Return of Colm:

"As usual, when I return to the Palace, I undergo a period of total and absolute Confusion. My normal modes of living are completely ineffectual for contacting other Atlanteans, and with all the good will in the world, I seem to have reached an impasse. All I can do is give up, become seemingly completely dependent on the whims, wishes, moods and desires of Atlantis and resign myself to my worst possible fears, the terrible fate

I have imagined will befall me. I assume I am going to be led blindfold into my most obvious blocks and stuckness. I imagine that I am already in a pit of resentment and hate for all Atlanteans who ever breathed on this Earth. I suppose all this – and a funny thing happens.

No-one notices I'm in a pit and everybody is laughing and happy, including myself. My worst worries have been and gone and I didn't even notice the event. What a let-down! Still, after a day or so, I'm sure more will come up so I can worry afresh.

And so, living in the Palace continues. I learn to give in to my fears and damn it! but when I do, they're not there. I'm fooling myself all along – with reason too: better to face a self-made fear than what really does lurk beneath the darkness, a thing so terrible I can't think of it, so terrible that its vaguest stirring sends me into a cold sweat.

Jenny and Becky and Snowy are doing psychic readings of people, including myself. Each time, I'm keyed up and prepared to face some terrific exposé of what my life is about. The readings are full of energy: a full person revealed, undefended by their usual blocks and hang-ups appears in the room. I set myself on guard for the intense involvement of a reading and over and over again, I am floored, too scared to actually relate to whoever is alive in the room. I miss all those chances, opportunities I so much want to move and to grow. One thing stands clear to me from all the readings: every person is a complete book of knowledge, each with a character, able to show and teach if only I could ask the right questions. I'm trying too hard, and my true way is to give in, to accept. I do, and damn it again, I find there is no wallowing in grovel and dependency after all. By accepting, I'm stronger. Atlantis is the inevitable, and when I don't fight the inevitable, I have more energy to have fun with.

I slowly learn to step down from my high horse without (1) breaking my ankle or (2) letting go the horse. I am given a beautiful vision of myself by Snowy's psychic reading of me: that of a man walking down a road to reveal treasures and riches for display to the world. It's strange sitting across the room, looking at yourself.

But I can go no further down the road to richness and fullness if I cannot yet walk. I must make my first step and to do that, I quite simply have to stand on one leg until my other foot goes down again. That's the picture. The fact of the matter is that on one of my first attempts to walk, I fell down flat on my face and was so upset, I refused to get up again. Fairy palaces are not mental hospitals, nor institutions for particularly sulky children. Fairies are not like other humans. As I just sat there waiting to be picked up, I noticed the fairies moving on away from me to their next dancing place, and feasting in another banqueting hall. I felt lumpy and swollen just sitting there, but the hall I was in was rather splendid and contained lots of memories and smells from the past.

But the torches dimmed and the laughter and song seemed to follow behind the fairies; the magic moved on too, and I grew cold sitting in my stone cottage, waiting for my fairies to dance their round again. But fairies never dance the same dance again and never sing the same song and all the time as I sat and waited, I grew greyer and colder, until I knew that even if the fairies came back, they would regard me with disgust. I felt ashamed of how I had been and stole away to places where no-one knew how I had behaved, places where I could forget the magic fairy dances and the shimmering lights, where I could forget myself.

Unfortunately, I could hardly forget Me when everywhere I went, there was Me close behind, treading on my heels, tripping me up, causing a lot of bother and trouble and not letting me get on with my normal sensible kind of life which I know and love so well. Me wouldn't leave me alone.

Eventually, Me has the fantastic cheek to come out from behind me and lead me back up the road from where me had taken Me. And so once again, I'm going up to the awesome entrance to my fairy palace. Surely, they must be fed up with me by now?

There are two Queens, the dark one, Queen of bright light and air; and her sister, Queen of Earth and Flames. A princess too, of dark smouldering passion and ancient knowledge; and I, a dusty wizard, weary and with half-forgotten magic. My pride has taken me away from there before, and now, broken and ashamed, I am come to heal my own wounds. My pained body is healing in the quiet flow of laughter and music. I am melting, my travel-hard body is cracking with the realization that there is nothing to defend against except what I have brought with me. My world-defences are not needed here, because my magic is at home and can be released to join the rippling waves of love.

I bathe myself, dress in coloured flowing robes and join with the fairies, kings and queens so old that they have seen the world unfolding time and time again beneath their eyes, wise with life and love and with a sadness of knowing that the world we have is not so unlike those we have had before. My self-inflicted exile has told on me, and my power, though stronger, is slower to rise.

One of the princesses suspects that we have Evil disguising itself as Faery in our midst. Evil is always drawn here, for it loves to devour and torment life at its sweetest. Strong magic is called for to expel the Beast. My wizardry is needed. Imagine a hunting beast scenting life-blood, and the snuffles and panting as he corners his quarry. By now, the beast was close and excited as he closed for the kill. But evil is blind. My spells were wide-eyed, and with woven magic, I brought the beast to scent me, till its head was filled only with lust for blood and for easy kill. I let it hunt close and blind, hunting for the wetness of life-blood. Then with my spells of excitement and blood-lust completed, I watched and waited for what I knew must happen. The beast, completely enflamed by its desire to devour, appeared from its faery disguise to ravage whatever flesh it could. But I had taken charge of all things living in the Palace, and protected them within my spell of Concealment. All the beast found was an empty hall, no scent but its own and the terrible knowledge that it had been tricked. The ever-elusive tinkle of faery music moved on and away, while the beast, left alone with only itself, slunk away, terror-struck behind its hate-blind eyes. I was a true Wizard again, welcome home amongst my people.

I discovered that strange rumours had been gathered by our messengers over the previous year. By the art of future-seeing, our dark Queen had found the present age to be drawing to a close, and she had been able to pinpoint more clearly how the age would end.

At the beginning of this Age, evil had been present in equal kind to the forces of Good, and a balance was kept in the favour of life. But as time slipped by, Man grew lazy and indulgent and no longer responded to the encroachment of Death in the realm of Life, rather preferring to enjoy what life he found, and not caring to create or renew. Death embedded itself in the hearts of men and natural ways were bent and twisted. The fairies knew now that it was too late to reverse the spread of evil: good men were too few and constantly in danger of their lives.

Earth was overrun by Death's forces and she would have no choice but to cleanse herself; and her purge, like those before, would be drastic. Within the faery realm, we knew well how to defend against evil, but we knew too, that in the cleansing of the Earth, we ourselves would be in danger from flood, fire and famine. Plans were being made therefore to build a magic ship on which we could board ourselves, our animals and plants, in order to carry our lives to safe havens. We had all our various skills: carpenters, ironsmiths and sailors; my wizardry to bind the ship firm and strong, and the magic of our faery kings and queens to conjure protection and safe voyage wherever we might roam.

The Palace was busy with excitement and preparation. Sorcery and wizardry drew sparks from the air. Emissaries came and went. The ship steadily took shape, until at last we were ready: the ship loaded, the Palace empty of its riches and finery, as we took our last leave of the world we had seen slip slowly across the centuries into decay and doom.

Such was our faery way, that though we made no secret of our flight, only those who sensed the joy of faery magic dared to join us. All others sank themselves more firmly into their dark pursuit of death in a world of misery and oblivion.

One year before the foreseen Collapse, we sailed away. One year we had to find safe haven from the catastrophes to come. We learnt to use our powers to sense storms, find favourable winds and currents, sighting land with the art of far-seeing.

It was a year of great Learning, for we communed with the beasts of the sea and learnt from them that they too, had a sense of foreboding. So with Dolphins as our guides, we brought ourselves to an ocean with many islands, each island a great mountain reaching high above the sea. We sailed to the tallest and transferred all in the boat, and then the boat itself, to the top of the mountain.

Nestling in the arms of the summit, was a valley, lush and protected by cliffs on all sides save the East. We built our home there with the materials from our ship and what was offered to us by Nature all around us. And then we waited with apprehension for what must soon come to pass.

That spring, the Earth moved. In the arms of our mountains, we were shaken but unhurt. We knew the Destruction had started. A great storm crashed and howled. The day turned into night and we felt the mountain tremble as great waves smashed against its sides. For forty days, there was no day, only howling, shrieking darkness. We despaired for an end, till suddenly, the Sun broke through and we could stare around us, bewildered and shaken to have survived such hell on Earth.

That night, a second moon rose in a cloudless sky, a moon smaller than the older moon, and the two spheres of light swept across the stars far slower than before. A new age had begun, and now we had the task of leading those who had survived out of the blackness and despair to stand tall and firmly rooted in harmony with Earth."